Cátedra México-China

THE RISE OF China's INDUSTRIAL POLICY 1978 TO 2020

Barry Naughton

THE RISE OF CHINA´S INDUSTRIAL POLICY, 1978-2020

Barry Naughton	*Autor*
Silvia Jiménez Barba	*Edición*
Socorro García	*Diseño y formación de interiores*

Primera edición: enero 2021
ISBN impreso: 978-607-8066-59-9
ISBN electrónico: 978-607-8066-60-5

Impreso y hecho en México/*Printed and made in Mexico*

THE RISE OF China's INDUSTRIAL POLICY 1978 TO 2020

Barry Naughton

CONTENTS

FOREWORD

The Center for Chinese-Mexican Studies (Cechimex) of the School of Economics of the National Autonomous University of Mexico (UNAM) is extremely happy and honoured to present the most recent research results of Barry Naughton.

The publication is part of the on-going efforts by Cechimex to make room —in a public dialogue with the public, private and academic sectors in Latin America and the Caribbean (LAC), China and other parts of the world— for a learning process with state-of-the-art analysis on China and of relevance for LAC. Since 2013, the Mexico-China Professorship Eugenio Anguiano Roch has been a reflection of these goals. Professor Naughton was invited in February of 2018 to participate in a group of activities in Mexico City —presentations in the academic, private and public sectors— to discuss specificities on China's development model and "growth miracle" since the reform and opening period at the end of the 1970s in light of his research and publications. The present book is an explicit result of these activities and further analysis since then.

The book, organized in six chapters, could be of utmost interest for readers from several perspectives. On the one hand, for those interested in China *per se* and particularly in understanding China's most recent economic performance; the respective chapters are full of references and detailed discussions that might be useful for specialized research. On the other hand, Barry's thoughts are also relevant for researchers, academics and policy makers who have an interest on economic development, overall economic upgrading and in specific sectors, trade and on industrial policy. Professor Naughton's analysis, from this perspective, is a valuable conceptual and empirical contribution regarding the recent genesis of industrial policy in China in the 21st century. Finally, the book also provides strong arguments —also for those interested in international relations and global issues— for understanding China's future in the global economy and in its tense relationship with the United States and other nations, including LAC.

We can only invite the readers to engage and participate critically in the activities of Cechimex since the early 2000s in order to improve the quality of analysis on China and the LAC-China relationship; there are massive contributions on a variety of topics presented in LAC, China and other countries, as well as by other public, private and academic institutions.

Finally, Cechimex wishes to congratulate and thank Agendasia and Simón Levy-Dabbah for endorsing this Chair; so far it is a unique contribution to the LAC-China understanding and we are looking forward to expounding on these activities in the future.

Enrique Dussel Peters
Coordinator
Center for Chinese-Mexican Studies
School of Economics
UNAM

1

Introduction: What Is Industrial Policy? What Is China's Industrial Policy?

China has rapidly emerged to become a large economy and a technological power. Although still a middle-income country, China now has the world's second most important high-tech sector, as well as the world's largest manufacturing and internet sectors. These are remarkable achievements by any standard. Moreover, just as recognition of China's developmental success has spread, China's leadership has begun to demand a greater international "voice," and a more prominent place for China in the global system. These enormous changes are placing huge demands on the resilience and adaptability of the world system, and at the same time on our understanding and ability to analyze accurately. Remarkable economic success provokes responses on an international level, but also domestically, as Chinese policy-makers react to new capabilities and opportunities. With so many factors changing at once, it is hard to pin down the drivers of change.

A question of particular importance is this: To what extent can China's undeniable economic and technological success be reasonably attributed to specific policies, and more generally to a Chinese "path," or program of industrial policy? China is big and complex, so from a distance it is natural to assume that many elements of policy are successful, in essence, the idea that "they must be doing something right." To be sure, China has done many things right. Therefore, it is essential to dive deeper and discriminate among a vast range of policies, in order to ask the question of what it is that China has done right. This volume makes a contribution to that process by disentangling specific threads of China's economic development policies over the past forty years. The objective is not to try to evaluate the effectiveness of specific policies, but simply to reliably track what policy was in effect during different periods, and where we might expect to see large and important impacts.

Since 1978, the beginning of China's period of "reform and opening," market-oriented system reform and openness to the outside world have been the most prominent features of China's policy orientation. Through the early years of the 21st century, market transition was undoubtedly the overwhelming focus of Chinese policy-makers. Even then, policy was gradual and incremental, and also exceptionally mutable, tackling different issues at different times, and moving forward sometimes faster, sometimes slower. Over the long term, taking into account all these policy shifts and turns of direction, China did extremely well, achieving unprecedented success. Moreover, there is little debate about the nature and cause of this achievement: China shifted to a market economy, growth accelerated, and rapid structural and technological upgrading followed.

Less widely appreciated, however, is that from about 2006, China began to make further fundamental shifts in development strategy. Direct government intervention in the economy —which had dwindled to almost nothing in the years 1998-2005— gradually began to increase. This shift at first attracted little attention. It came after a period of minimal government intervention in the sectoral structure of the economy, as policy-makers had focused on creating the institutional infrastructure of a market economy, solving the problems of state-owned enterprises, and joining the World

Trade Organization. As those things were being accomplished, it was not surprising that policy-makers shifted attention to fixing things that were not working (such as health insurance and rural taxation) and also toward shaping policy for the next phase of growth. Besides, the changes were at first quite modest. As is described in Chapter 3, beginning in 2006, China promulgated a series of policies and programs that represented the launch of its modern industrial policies. From that point, China, with increasing determination, began to increase the level of direct government intervention. During the Global Financial Crisis (GFC), as part of a massive stimulus program, China dramatically increased direct government intervention and the experience gave policy-makers increasing confidence in their new path.

This new Chinese government effort expanded just as the Chinese economy was slowing. To be sure, the new policy package was a *response* to the slowdown, not the cause of it. In the 1980s and 1990s, market reforms had coincided with China's highest growth potential, as under-employed farmers migrated to new rural and urban occupations and China enjoyed a massive demographic dividend. Now, policy-makers were searching for —in their favorite phrase— "new growth drivers."[1] In addition, from about 2015-2016, it became clear that artificial intelligence and big data had huge potential economic effects on economies worldwide. As technological change has accelerated, the ambition of China's planners and policy-makers has also expanded, and intervention has continued and increased. Indeed, China's development strategy today may warrant a new name: China aspires to be the first "government-steered market economy."

These dramatic changes need to be better understood. This essay contributes to this understanding by tracing the different stages through which Chinese industrial policy and planning have passed through over the last forty years. It will immediately become clear from this review that there is a great difference between China's development strategy and outcomes between two long periods.

1 For these broad changes, see Naughton (2018: chapters 1, 6, 7, and 8).

Between 1978 and about 2005, China's government steadily retreated from its initially all-encompassing control of the economy, growth accelerated, and comprehensive upgrading took place. New policies began to be initiated in 2006, starting slow and then accelerating. From 2009 through 2020, the government has strongly re-engaged in direct economic intervention, all while the economy has been steadily slowing (even before the coronavirus impact in 2020). To be sure, there is not a cause and effect relation between government intervention and economic slowdown, and it is also true that the slowdown has led policy-makers to increase their intervention. Nonetheless, there is a huge disconnect between the success that we attribute to the Chinese economy today and the orientation of Chinese policy today. China's emergence as an economic and technological super-power is due primarily to the policy package that it followed from 1978 through the first decade of the 21st century, that is, until about 2006-7. China's policy package *today* —that is, the policies that started tentatively after 2005 but were fully in place by 2008-2010— are radically different. Because of this, it is a mistake to attribute China's success to the policies China is currently following. These policies are simply too recent to have had a determinative impact on today's outcomes. China is a technological superpower because it followed smart policies after 1978, pursuing marketization and investment in human and physical capital. Whether or not the industrial policies that have been followed in the most recent decade will contribute to China's technological and economic prowess is not yet clear. This distinction is particularly important as a newly assertive China, under Xi Jinping, calls for a "China road" that deserves recognition in the global marketplace of ideas, and yet rarely, if ever, specifies what the elements are that make up this "China road."

1.1. Setting Aside Three Misconceptions

It will help in our discussion of Chinese development policy if we set aside from the outset three important misconceptions. It is not that these are completely false conceptions: they are rather over-simplifications that contain some element of truth and might be partially defended using certain definitions. But each of them represents an easy assumption about reality that ends up obstructing a clear view of Chinese policy, and indeed of the uniqueness of the current Chinese effort. It will be best if the reader temporarily sets these conceptions aside in order to focus on what is distinctive about Chinese policy today.

1.1.1. China is NOT Just Another East Asian Developmental State

One often hears that China is following an industrial policy rather similar to that followed by Japan, Korea, and other earlier fast developing East Asian economies, so-called "developmental states." This is wrong in multiple dimensions. On one hand, China inherited a legacy of total government control when it entered the contemporary era. To be sure, that government control, as of 1978, was completely dysfunctional. However, precisely because the command economy was so distorted, policy-makers had to give all their attention to implementing market reform without blowing up the economy; they had no conceptual space nor effective instruments for implementing Japan-style industrial policy. While Japan and Korea layered industrial policy on top of reviving war-shattered economies, those economies were primarily market-based and small-scale. China's starting point was precisely the opposite, and it spent thirty years throwing off the legacy of excessive direct government control.

On the other hand, China's new industrial policies, since about 2010, have been very different from those of Japan and Korea. The volume of resources the Chinese state invests in targeted sectors has been *much* greater than anything Japan or Korea ever invested, both as a share of the economy and even more so in absolute dollar amounts. Likewise, the nature of the targeting is also completely different. Japan and Korea steered the economy to *catch-up*, in clearly defined sectors where the objective was to match the performance of industry leaders (in Germany or the US); in China, the main focus has been on *leap-frog*, in the sense that the most heavily prioritized sectors have been those emerging areas where the technological leadership is less clear and there are few entrenched incumbents in developed economies. These differences are so large that to think of Chinese industrial policies as fundamentally similar phenomena to earlier Japanese and Korean industrial policies can only lead to confusion.

1.1.2. There is NO Definable "Chinese Road"

Chinese policy-makers, headed by Party General Secretary Xi Jinping, have recently taken to declaring that there is a "Chinese road" to development that may hold lessons for other developing economies. In his official report to the 19th Communist Party Congress in October 2017, Xi Jinping said that China's approach "offers a new option for other countries who want to speed up their development while preserving their independence" (Xi 2017). In one sense, this is completely unobjectionable. China is an enormous, diverse economy, and between 1978 and 2010 it grew faster, for longer, than any economy in human history. Of course, there are lessons for development from China, indeed, many lessons from China. There is already a large academic literature on those lessons, extending from economics through sociology to health care, and many others. However, one of the common findings of these discussions is precisely that the distinctiveness of Chinese institutions, and especially the dominance of the Communist Party, means that transferability of successful experience is difficult.[2]

2 See: Kennedy (2010) and Naughton (2019). Indeed, to the extent that there is an official Chinese definition of the "Chinese road," it is "market socialism with Chinese characteristics" which is defined as an adaptation of socialist theory to specific Chinese conditions, thus implying that other countries should make their own, rather different, adaptations.

Partly as a result of these concerns, most talk about a "Chinese road" today satisfies itself with an overly simple, abstract formulation that does not specify what, if anything, the lessons of the Chinese road are. For example, I have been told more than once by Chinese scholars that "close government-business cooperation" is the essence of the Chinese model. But such a formulation does not differentiate China from many other less successful economies that also have "close government-business cooperation." As a result, such a formulation really does not tell us anything that is useful as a "lesson." Moreover, it doesn't describe very well *any* of the achievements of Chinese economic growth and development over the past forty years.

1.1.3. Conflict Among Technological Powers is NOT Inevitable

Many people attribute the rise in conflict between China and other nations —not least the United States— to an inevitable "Thucydides trap," or competition between a rising "challenger" and a jealous incumbent. This view is not completely wrong, but it is hopelessly over-simplified. One simple fact is that the incidence of conflict increased dramatically following the acceleration of China's industrial policy. The magnitude of China's intervention in emerging sectors has seriously disrupted international norms and agreements about the nature of economic and technological competition. This doesn't necessarily mean that China is "wrong." Some of those norms might be cozy agreements between comfortable entrenched powers, and might indeed be ripe for re-consideration and revision. But it is not unreasonable for us to ask that China —along with other "revisionist" powers— clarify which norms and agreements they want to see changed. In the meantime, we can reject out of hand the idea that China was simply pursuing some kind of relatively consistent "Chinese way" when controversy suddenly erupted because of criticism and countermeasures from the United States. That just doesn't fit the most basic facts. Instead, the world is faced with a more complex challenge: hammering out a set of rules and principles that will allow great powers to compete with each other without spiraling down into intensifying conflict.

1.2. Defining Industrial Policy

In this essay, I use a relatively narrow definition of industrial policy. This is not the only possible definition, nor is it the best definition for all purposes. An alternative, broader definition would also have some benefits, because it might help us identify some common features across countries and also compare and contrast very different countries in a systemic way. For example, Knight (2014) calls China a "developmental state," using a broad definition that permits him to focus on the presence of an overarching national goal of economic development, as well as an incentive structure that rewards government officials for pursuing growth (Knight 2014). This very effectively draws out the commonalities between China, Japan, and Korea in their high growth eras, while leaving the differences to one side. In another sense, a broad definition allows authors to bring in regulation, fiscal and monetary policy, and innovation and human resource policy. For example, Brandt and Rawski (2019) use a broad definition to bring multiple perspectives to bear on the electrical sector, among others, showing the complex relations between regulation, competition policy, and direct sectoral intervention (Brandt and Rawski 2019).

However, the use of a broad definition requires a great deal of additional discussion about what should or should not be included, and in the end that broader debate is better conducted with some agreement on basic facts. Without additional specification, the broad definition leads to statements like "all countries have industrial policies," or "the real question about industrial policy is not whether it should be practiced, but how" (Rodrik 2012:53-56). These statements aren't wrong (if a broad definition is used), but they are only a first step in getting to an understanding of what the consequences of specific policies are. Similarly, Justin Lin's support for "industrial policy" based on an effective government and a market economy can be useful, but depends on a very broad understanding of what industrial policy includes (Lin 2012). The following discussion is based on the proposition that further analysis can be facilitated by pursuing a narrow but clear definition of industrial policy. The use of this definition contributes to discussion not because it is the only correct definition, but because it can be clearly specified, and thus lead us to clear conclusions.

Industrial policy is used consistently in this book to mean an intentional effort on the part of government policy-makers to change the sectoral structure of the economy. Industrial policies are adopted when government identifies and actively supports industries that contribute to growth. Industrial policy in this sense presupposes a market economy, and it only makes sense to consider industrial policy in that context.[3] In a dynamic context, the government's targets dynamic sectors in order that they make a bigger contribution to growth than they otherwise would. More precisely, I define industrial policy as follows:

> Industrial policy is any type of selective, targeted government intervention that attempts to alter the sectoral structure of production toward sectors that are expected to offer better growth than would occur in the (non-interventionist) market equilibrium.[4]

It only makes sense to talk about industrial policy if real resources are devoted to selective interventions that policy-makers make

3 Ever since 1949, through a variety of systems and instruments, the Chinese government has attempted to drive/guide the economic development process and shape the particular pattern of industrialization. However, from 1949 into the 1980s, those interventions were carried out as part of the "command economy," an entirely different system without a market basis on which to operate an industrial policy. Indeed, in the command economy, the word "planning" refers primarily to the actions bureaucrats take managing day to day transactions among units of the economy, often leaving them little time to develop strategic and technologically dynamic sectors. Not until the growth of a market economy does it become meaningful to speak of "industrial policy" *per se*.

4 Based on, but significantly altered from, the definition in Pack and Kamal (2006:2).

and they have real instruments available to shape the incentives of economic decision-makers. Simply stating a desired or expected outcome does not constitute an industrial policy, even if that statement is issued by an authoritative body, like the State Planning Commission. For example, Deng Xiaoping in 1982 declared that China should quadruple GDP by 2000, and both Hu Jintao and Xi Jinping have since declared that China will quadruple GDP again by 2020. These do not constitute industrial policy, although they may serve other purposes by mobilizing national effort and articulating collective aspirations. In a different sense, China began promulgating what it called "Industrial Policies" in the 1990s, but those efforts rarely had any real resources behind them. For example, successive Automobile Industrial Policies called for the concentration of production in three main producers, and the upgrading and expansion of these three state-owned enterprises (with some limited foreign investment to help). However, nothing like this ever happened, unsurprisingly, since planners had no resources or instruments to carry out their desires, and the actual evolution of the auto industry bore no relation at all to their wishes. I do not consider this an industrial policy.[5] To be classified as an industrial policy, there has to be an actual intervention into the real economy. Words that remain on paper do not count as an intervention, absent some real actions that have an impact.

After all these clarifications and caveats, we find that a narrow definition of industrial policy allows us to make a very clear and unambiguous statement about Chinese industrial policy. Moreover, this statement is surprising and simple, yet easily supported and defended:

> Until 2006, China never had "industrial policy." Since about 2010, China has had industrial policy on a massive and unprecedented scale. The outcomes of post-2010 industrial policy in China have not been adequately studied and are as yet unknown.

5 The alternative, of course, would be to consider this a failed industrial policy. But since the policies had little cost, as well as little impact, there does not seem to be any point in doing this.

The remaining chapters in this volume will provide the justification for this strong statement. However, before moving on we need to introduce further clarification of what is, and is not, part of industrial policy.

1.3. The Impact of Industrial Policy

Evaluating the outcome and impact of industrial policy is challenging. There is no consensus about the impact of industrial policy in Japan or Korea, even though those economies ended their experiments with government industrial policy decades ago and have relatively good data available. Such an effort is far more difficult than anything attempted in this essay. In part, the difficulty comes from clearly distinguishing and measuring the various steps in industrial policy. It makes sense to discriminate between three stages: resource effort (magnitude), sectoral impact, and efficiency.

The resource effort involved in an industrial policy —which I refer to as "magnitude" for short— refers to the actual cost of a policy. This should include the direct cost of subsidies and preferential tax treatment plus the indirect cost of regulatory barriers and protectionist policies used to nurture a targeted sector. The magnitude of industrial policy is the sum of the resources actually spent plus the resource cost of market distortions induced by government interventions.[6] Cost is not in itself a bad thing: The most successful interventions will not have been costless. Cost is, however, hard to measure, particularly in China where so many different overlapping instruments have been applied to support core industrial policy objectives. At this point, the most we can say is that there is strong evidence that the overall cost (resource effort) of China's industrial policy increased dramatically between 2006 and 2018.

6 In principle, measured at shadow prices. The 1990s Automobile Industrial Policy is dropped from consideration because its direct costs were zero and its indirect costs, while hard to measure, are unlikely to have been significant.

The sectoral impact of industrial policy refers to the magnitude of the effects of industrial policy. That is, we ask how much the composition of the economy (alternatively, of economic growth) shifted in the direction that planners envisioned. Did semiconductor industry policy result in faster growth of semiconductor production than would otherwise have occurred? This question is difficult because the counter-factual is hard to know: what would the trajectory of the economy have been in the absence of intervention? Presumably industrial policy-makers are smart enough to target promising industries that would have grown faster than average in any case, and if planners see that a sector is likely to be lucrative in the future, aren't there visionary entrepreneurs who see the same? We can benchmark future performance against industrial policy plan targets, but we do not really know the intentions of policy-makers, and this risks unfairly penalizing planners for promulgating over-ambitious targets that may have been costless. Another possibility is to use performance proxies, such as global market share for specific industries, or the presence of recognized leading global companies, to measure impact.

The efficiency of industrial policy is determined by comparison of the cost of the policy with the additional output that was produced. In other words, what was the rate of return of the investment in industrial policy? Since our measures of costs and impact are both weak, it follows that our ability to measure the efficiency of industrial policy will be even weaker. It is striking that in the vast descriptive literature on China's industrial policy, there scarcely exists a case study that argues that a specific industrial policy has been a conspicuous success. However, this could be due to time lags, since massive industrial policy is quite recent.[7] Finally, in the presence of major spillovers from one sector to another, it may be too limiting to try to assess the impact of industrial policy on a single sector. Perhaps the positive impact will be captured in other

7 However, there have been some good studies of the impact of specific instruments through 2006 (Boeing 2016).

sectors that benefit from cheaper and more accessible inputs from local suppliers.

Thus, the questions involved in the evaluation of industrial policy are hard to answer under the best of circumstances, and impossible in the Chinese case, given the current state of our knowledge. In this essay, I will mainly be concerned with showing the dramatic changes over time in the resource effort put into China's industrial policy. I am somewhat skeptical that the enormous costs of these policies is being, or will be, realized in better performance, but I acknowledge that the data are not good enough to say anything definitive. The ultimate outcome is unknown. China is gam bling an enormous amount on the outcome of a new technological revolution, but the outcome of that gamble is not yet known.

1.4. What is *NOT* Industrial Policy?

Adopting a narrow definition of industrial policy inevitably means that many things that are very important to economic and technological development are excluded. Indeed, these excluded things are, in my view, even more important than industrial policy in explaining China's extraordinary development. But precisely for that reason, they should not be mixed up with the discussion about industrial targeting. In particular, I wish to exclude all "horizontal" policies, that is, policies that may foster economic development but do so without prejudice as to which particular sectors will grow. Horizontal policies are non-targeted interventions, because they effect all businesses and sectors more-or-less the same. By my definition, industrial policy is vertical, involving targeting of specific sectors. In particular, I identify three things that industrial policy in China is NOT:

1. Industrial policy is *not* intensive investment in infrastructure. China since about 1996, has invested large amounts in infrastructure, in many cases "building out ahead of demand." Overall, China's investment rate is extremely high, far

higher than any other country today, or ever. China's fixed investment (of all types, not just infrastructure) as a share of GDP has been well over 40% since 2009. This obviously has extremely important effects on China's development. It has big benefits, and also huge costs. If physical infrastructure construction were included in our definition of industrial policy, its economic effects would almost certainly overshadow everything else. Moreover, there is virtually unanimous agreement that governments should invest in physical infrastructure: provision of public goods through infrastructure is a core government responsibility. All governments, except for failed states, provide some level of infrastructure construction. Therefore, the important discussion about China's infrastructure investment is limited in scope: Is China investing the right amount in infrastructure? Is it too much? Will China see economic returns from the hundreds of billions of dollars invested in modern infrastructure? The ultimate objective of economic policy is to enhance the well-being of the population over the long-run, and investment contributes to this if and only if the investment is productive enough to provide future benefits that more than compensate for the current cost in foregone consumption.

High physical investment rates certainly influence the industrial policy environment. High infrastructure spending corresponds with high government purchasing power, giving it the ability to give larger aggregate procurement preferences to priority firms and technologies. Thus, high levels of infrastructure spending act as a kind of "force multiplier" for industrial policies. Moreover, in China, many of the firms most active in provision of infrastructure construction are state-owned enterprises. Many of these firms have been encouraged to engage in a long-term and ambitious upgrading effort, as they have absorbed advanced construction techniques from the world. China, once decades behind, is now at the frontier of construction technique. The process of upgrading in these firms has not been well studied, and should count as a type of industrial policy, but at this point it is not distinguishable from the impact of high infrastructure investment in itself.

2. Industrial policy is *not* investment in human resources. Since the turn of the century, China has invested a great deal in higher education and in research facilities.[8] In addition, China has encouraged students to go abroad for higher education, and given them a remarkable degree of latitude in deciding whether to pursue careers abroad or in China. Although the majority of post-graduate students have remained overseas, enough have returned to China to significantly expand China's human capital base. What is more, the returning students have been especially active in entrepreneurial activities, accounting for a disproportionate share of China's most dynamic enterprises. There is no question that China's investment in human resources —and encouragement to families to invest in their children's human capital— has been a major contributor to China's technological catch-up. These investment in China's human resource base are quintessentially "horizontal": that is, they improve the capabilities of the Chinese economy across the board, without preference to any particular sector.

This type of knowledge investment probably comes closest to industrial policy in the area of state-sponsored research and development projects, many of which have direct military applications. With military-civilian fusion being a long-term trend in China's military industrial management system —and a specific military-civilian plan adopted in 2017— Chinese defense investments have obvious spillover effects on industry, particularly given that state-owned

8 Investment in pure knowledge can be conceptually separated from investment in human capital, but there is no need to do so in this case. To begin with, until the present, very little Chinese investment has been made in pure science, and until very, very recently, even the most advanced research and development was essentially directed at bringing Chinese researchers to the global frontier, thus being human capital investments rather than pure knowledge investments.

firms are still dominant in the defense industry sectors. Still, on balance, it makes sense to treat the defense sector as a special case, driven primarily by non-economic considerations, and through the present having a relatively small presence in the overall economy.

3. The existence of a local "developmental state" is not *ipso facto* evidence of industrial policy. Clearly, a distinctive feature of the Chinese economy since the late 1970s has been the active engagement of local governments in fostering economic development (Oi 1992). Local government entrepreneurship and investment in local public goods are certainly important features of China's developmental model, and contributed to China's rapid growth during its "miracle growth" phase (1978-2010). However, China has tens of thousands of local governments, all engaged in expanding economic activity. They have to compete with each other in the marketplace, and are under great pressure to generate new revenues. In short, they behave more like firms than like governments in this respect, and it is hard to see how they aggregate into a pattern of government-sponsored development that is different from firms seeking profit through the market. Indeed, the influential model of "market-preserving federalism" essentially characterizes local governments as being forced by competition to abstain from market-distorting policies; this essentially disqualifies them from being agents of government-sponsored industrial policies (Montinola, Qiaan and Weingast 1995; Xu 2011). To be sure, there is a grey area, where some of the larger local governments, such as the central municipalities of Beijing and Shanghai, articulate true industrial policies, targeting promising sectors and promoting "local heroes." I will strive to include those initiatives where appropriate, while continuing to exclude generic local governments from the industrial policy story.

Readers may object that I am excluding some of the most important aspects of Chinese development strategy from my discussion of industrial policy, but that is precisely the point. Powerful targeted industrial policies in China have been generally absent (1978-2005) and have sometimes been overbearing (2010-present), but they have never been a crucial component in explaining rapid Chinese economic growth. That doesn't mean that government doesn't matter, or that distinctive Chinese approaches have not been important: it does, and they have been. Indeed, it should be intuitively obvious that the impact of a large-scale fixed investment effort, massive investment in human resources, and the presence of thousands of growth-promoting local governments competing with each other will be much greater than the impact of government efforts to directly intervene in the sectoral development pattern of the economy. Of course, these are not mutually exclusively choices. But targeted industrial policy is still utterly unproven in terms of its impact on China's development. It may turn out, 20 years from now, to have been a huge success, but as of today, there is very little evidence for its importance or success.

Readers who favor a more expansive definition of industrial policy are still welcome to use it. For those who insist on this more expansive definition, the argument of this essay could be easily restated as follows: China's overall industrial policies have been very effective in promoting economic development, but among those policies, the impact of targeted industrial policy interventions has been small, and perhaps zero or even negative. For all that, it is important to unravel the various parts of the story in order to have a clear view of China's overall development strategy.

1.5. Plan of the Essay

This essay is organized in chronological fashion. That means that readers who are most interested in today's industrial policies in China may wish to jump immediately to Chapter 4, which describes the rationale and magnitude of the "Innovation-Driven

Development Strategy" (IDDS), that was formally adopted in 2016, and Chapter 5, which describes the specific tools and instruments used to carry out the IDDS. Those interested in tracking the development of China's approach to industrial policy and planning should continue straight on to Chapter 2, which discusses planning in the period from 1978 through the early 2000s, showing the extremely inconsistent nature of that planning, the reasons for its diminishing importance overall, and some of the lessons Chinese policy-makers may have gleaned from it. Chapter 3 describes the turning point, the gradual turn to techno-industrial policy that was initiated by Wen Jiabao shortly after he became premier in 2003, but was first formalized as policy in 2006. This then became the most important component of economic development policy after the 2008 Global Financial Crisis. Chapter 4 describes the way current industrial policy has changed in response to the perception of accelerating technological change. Sector-specific industrial policies have now been grouped together under the rubric of the Innovation-Driven Development Strategy. Chapter 5 then discusses in more detail the instruments and institutions developed as part of the IDDS. They underscore the novelty and ambition of the IDDS. This also justifies why I argue that the "government-steered market economy" (articulated by Chinese policy-makers) is taking shape as a distinctive set of institutions and deserves to be considered as a new type of economic system. While it is far too early to judge the feasibility or efficiency of this system, it is at least a new phenomenon of which note should be taken. A brief conclusion summarizes the main insights gained in the course of writing this essay.

2

Bringing the Economy to Life: Growth without Industrial Policy

The Chinese era of economic reform began at the crucial "Third Plenum" meeting in December 1978. At this meeting, a new political configuration was on display and it signaled the beginning of a new era of market reform and economic opening. It is equally true, if much less remarked, that this meeting also signaled the abandonment of a specific economic plan and development strategy. Chinese policy-makers did not decide to move away from the planned economy in general, they made a much more specific, concrete —and painful— decision to abandon a particular plan. The beginnings of market-oriented reform in China were inextricably linked to this concrete decision. In fact, this type of action occurred repeatedly during the reform era (1978-2005), as plans and industrial policies were proposed—only to be ultimately discarded as unrealistic, unfeasible, or dysfunctional. It is worth recounting some of these successive attempts, as they form the common learned experience of Chinese policy-makers and planners.

The first part of this chapter describes the pattern of unrealistic planning that led to the repeated proposal and abandonment of plans. As unrealistic plans were discarded, new approaches to planning were proposed and these are briefly discussed: such initiatives are worthy of note as "sprouts" that were developed much later, they do not change the basic picture described earlier. Next, I ask what actually mattered to the changing structure of the economy. After all, if planning and industrial policy were not ushering structural change and growth, what was? In fact, once posed, the answer to this question is obvious. The process of market reform —which took place at different paces in different sectors— drove the process of structural change. In other words, the uneven progress of "enlivening" the economy determined outcomes. Sectors that were "enlivened" grew more rapidly, and this unbalanced process drove growth and development. Finally, by the late 1990s, a "new normal" had emerged, as policy-makers and planners absorbed their experience over the previous two decades and focused on the development of a more efficient market economy. Premier Zhu Rongji took important steps to build the institutions behind this market economy, and he all but abandoned efforts to shape the economy through plans and industrial policy. There was every reason to expect that this "new normal" would be a stable attribute of China's economy. However, as the following chapter makes clear, this was not to be the case.

2.1. A Series of Failed Plans

Chinese policy-makers have been repeatedly tempted by two ambitious goals: rapid growth and restored economic order. Neither of those ideal goals is unreasonable. The Chinese economy has in fact been characterized by tremendous growth potential, and at the same time institutional distortions and macroeconomic imbalances have led to repeated episodes of imbalance and disorder. However, the desire to achieve these contrasting ideals has led to extremely unrealistic plans, particularly during the first 20 years of the reform era. As a result, a pattern of unfulfilled and ultimately discarded plans has characterized most of the post-1978 period.

2.1.1. The Planning Failure that Began the Reform Era

When China entered the crucial year of 1978, it had an operational development strategy that had been carried over from the period before the death of Mao Zedong. That strategy was embodied in the Ten-Year Plan (covering 1976-1985), which had been formulated in 1975. This was a modified heavy-industry-first strategy. At the core was development of the steel and chemical industries. The purpose of the modifications was to foster industrial developments that would target the agricultural bottleneck by providing agricultural machinery, fertilizer, and pesticides to farmers. The plan was formulated in two stages: first, create a basically self-sufficient industrial system by 1980, including "basically realizing agricultural mechanization." In the second stage, between 1980 and 1985, growth would accelerate, six distinctive regional industrial systems would take shape, and the "Four Modernizations" would be under way (Liu 2006). Interrupted by the succession struggle following the death of Mao, this plan was resurrected in 1977 as the framework for the rehabilitation of the economy. As part of the program, China planned to step up the import of equipment embodying modern technology and pay for it with petroleum exports. The initial draft of the program, in July 1977, proposed importing $6.5 billion worth of new industrial plants in the eight years from 1978 through 1985.

This initial plan had a certain coherence. As China began to open up in 1977-78, policy-makers sought to carry through the plan while opening more rapidly to the outside world and accelerating the import of foreign technology. In successive meetings, the import target was doubled, and then doubled again. In the summer of 1978, the State Council held a series of "theory-oriented" meetings that approved a total import program of $80 billion (through 1985) (Li 2010). In only a year, the scale of anticipated import increased more than ten times! In practice, the expansion of import plans was completely unrealistic, and at the end of 1978, the program suddenly imploded. Only after that program had collapsed did China begin to make the irreversible steps that would transform it into a predominantly market economy —and the most successful economy in the world— over the next thirty years.

This plan was inflated by the extreme high hopes of the Chinese leaders, fueled by their visits abroad after the long isolation of the Cultural Revolution. Projects were greenlit without real project planning or serious economic analysis. Each of the several hundred large projects should have gone through a rigorous process of site selection and preparation, financing selection, and supply decision, none of which actually happened. Even the flagship Baoshan Steel Mill in Shanghai, expected to be the pioneer and proof of concept, ran into substantial problems with site preparation and supply coordination. In addition, the program was extremely risky, since China had essentially no foreign exchange reserves, and payment depended on export earnings, primarily of petroleum.[1] During 1978, China's petroleum ministry discovered it would not be able to increase its exports of oil at all. The ten-year plan had projected 1985 crude oil production at 250 million metric tons (MMT); but actual production turned out to be exactly half of this (125 MMT). In fact, China's crude oil output has never reached the 1985 target, and probably never will.[2] The poor planning that characterized the technology import program was revealed to have been endemic in domestic industry as well. These short term problems brought down the import program at the end of 1978.

Even more relevant, the technology import program was premised on the idea that imported technology could provide a "quick fix" to the economy, without making the far more fundamental

1 According to corrected foreign reserve data subsequently released, China had only \$167 million in reserves at the end of 1978. This was enough to cover five and a half *days* of imports, while the "rule of thumb" for reserve adequacy is that reserves should cover three months-worth of imports. See NBS (2019:164) (or any post-1992 statistical source). In the adjustment of this program, China was able to shift some outlays to the credit of long-term suppliers.

2 Instead, crude oil output peaked thirty years later in 2015 at 215 MMT and has declined annually since.

—and difficult— changes in the economic system and strategy that were needed. For thirty years, China had been following a policy of extracting resources from the countryside and pumping them into heavy industry investment. This strategy of forced draft industrialization was not working well. What better way to resuscitate the faltering industrialization drive than to inject a massive dose of foreign machinery into China's factories? In fact, this program involved driving the domestic economy in precisely the wrong direction. Importing embodied industrial technology was part of a program of increasing domestic investment in heavy industry. Yet at this time the most urgent need was for China to increase food supply and buttress consumption. Together, the short-term and long-term problems with the plan effectively doomed it. Within days after the Third Plenum, the veteran leader Chen Yun regained control over economic policy, and he immediately instituted dramatic measures to cut back the plans for 1979 and 1980, knowing that this was equivalent to cutting the cord for the entire plan. Support for the Ten-Year Plan collapsed, and a completely different approach to economic development strategy emerged.

2.1.2. Subsequent Failed Plans

In the wake of this dramatic reorientation of the economy, the focus of policy-makers shifted to "reform," the difficult search for policies to carry out profound marketization. The heightened priority given to market reforms did not mean that planners became quiescent. They continued to produce regular five-year plans, but in an environment of extraordinary change. Each of the next three five-year plans —the 6th (1981-1985); 7th (1986-1990); and the 8th (1991-1995)— was an intentionally conservative undertaking. These plans were designed to tamp down the excessive "animal spirits" that tended to develop in the wake of reforms. The Sixth Five-Year Plan (1981-1985) called for continued slow growth, controls on investment so that consumption would grow at least as fast as total output, and concentration of investment on bottleneck sectors, particularly energy (Plan Chronology 1987; Liu 2006; Naughton 1990). Due to the conclusion that problems in energy production in particular were severe and required deep restructuring and extensive investment, output of bottleneck sectors was expected to increase relatively slowly. Output of electricity was planned to increase 20% over five years, and coal, China's main source of primary energy, only 13%. Oil production would not grow at all. Meanwhile, the planned increase in gross output over the five-year period was 22%. Improved energy utilization was a central part of the plan. The Sixth Plan sent clear messages that investment restraint would continue and that the supply of energy would not improve substantially. In practice, the economy grew far faster than this, largely because economic reform unleashed substantial productivity growth, and the structure of the economy shifted to much less energy-intensive light industry and services. In annual terms, planned growth for both industry and agriculture had been only 4%, while realized growth was 12% and 8% respectively. Obviously, planners had overshot in their effort to restrain investment, and were unable to commit to a stable, unchanged macroeconomic policy.

The Seventh Plan (1986-1990) was prepared in an orderly fashion, with planning exercises carried out throughout the bureaucracy and input-output matrices used for the first time to evaluate alternate projections (Chen 1989; Hamrin 1990:40-50, 119-138). The Seventh Plan was formulated in terms of gross national product for the first time, slated to grow 7.5% annually. Actual growth during the first three years of the Seventh Plan was substantially more rapid than envisaged, at 10% annually from 1985 to 1988, and most industrial output targets for 1990 were actually attained in 1988. But the Seventh Plan was still a poor predictor of the future: growth accelerated uncontrollably between 1985 and 1988, and then the brakes were pressed on hard before and after June 1989. Because the central government was unable to predict its own behavior in the sphere of macroeconomic policy, the plan as a whole turned out to be unrealistic. Chinese planning has been hampered by inconsistent and unpredictable behavior at the central government level, as well as political disruption (CCP Central Committee 1990).

In the Eighth Five-Year Plan (1991-1995), a re-empowered State Planning Commission saw itself as rectifying all the imbalances that had arisen during the 1980s, and the disruption caused by the political turbulence of 1989. It produced a Five-Year Plan that prioritized comprehensive rebalancing and "integration of plan and market," and a GDP growth rate of 6% annually, with worker wages growing 2% annually (Liu 2006:552, 557). Planners also envisioned a new program of investment in "basic industries," like that of the 1950s (and uncomfortably similar to those of the abandoned Ten-Year Plan of 1975-1985). However, the conservatives running the Planning Commission faced a fundamental problem: the issues they were most concerned about had pretty much disappeared by the end of 1990. Inflation was over —replaced by mild deflation in urban areas— while shortages of producer goods and electricity had evaporated. The conservatives had no real forward-looking program to implement for the next steps. The actual development of the economy in the plan period turned out to be nothing like what the planners expected. Stimulated by Deng Xiaoping's "Southern Tour" and the resumption of reform, growth was far higher than what planners anticipated. Annual GDP growth reached 12%, compared to just under 6% in the plan. GDP in 1995 was 76% greater than in 1990, instead of the 33.6% projected. The plan represented a kind of willful refusal to see what the economy was capable of, carried out by planners with ideological blinders that prevented them from seeing the economy's potential with market-oriented reform.

Thus, by the mid-1990s, each of the last four Five-Year Plans had been abandoned halfway through. Naturally, Chinese policymakers were aware of this failure, and the disillusionment with the planning process was virtually complete. Five-Year Plans were still announced for the 9th (1995-2000) and 10th (2001-2005) Periods, but they were very short and vague guidance documents. The compilers of the 9th Plan faced the challenge that the ambitious aspirational target for 2000 GDP, laid out by Deng Xiaoping in the previous decade, had already been achieved in 1995. The plan sidestepped the question of growth targets altogether, and instead put forward targets for labor productivity increase, investment rate, and energy utilization. The official Plan Outline mainly discussed the most urgent tasks facing the country, which it defined as controlling population growth, reforming state enterprises, reducing poverty, and redistributing growth toward inland regions (Guo 2006:858-1028). The 10th Plan (2001-2005) was even less specific, and explicitly stated that growth should be based on market signals and competition (Guo 2006:1030-1295). Thus, by the turn of the century, the traditional planning process had widely been seen to fail and was abandoned in all but name.

2.1.3. Discussion

The pattern of unrealistic plans, subsequently abandoned, was thus repeatedly in evidence between 1978 and 2000. In most cases, plans were discarded because the overall growth assumptions on which they were based —that is, the broad macroeconomic growth conditions of the economy— changed in ways that planners were unable to predict. Moreover, the changes in the economy wrought by market-oriented reforms were so profound that "planners" struggled to keep up with what had already changed in their economy. They did not even have the ability to forecast likely futures with any accuracy, much less shape those outcomes according to their will. Increasingly, they felt that the job of planners was simply to get out of the way.

2.2. Alternative Approaches

To be sure, during this period, the traditional Five-Year Plan cycle was not the only game in town. During the 1980s and 1990s, Japanese-style "industrial policy" was frequently cited as an objective for policy-makers to work toward (Heilmann and Shih 2013;

Heilmann and Oliver 2013:520-628). Industrial policy seemed to promise something for everyone. Japanese principles made it clear that firms constituted the basic decision-making units, and so the Japanese approach was attractive to market reformers who needed theoretical support for a further expansion of enterprise decision-making authority. At the same time, "industrial policy" seemed to promise planners a continued role and function in steering the economy toward desired outcomes and away from the worst manifestations of market irrationality. Indeed, at the end of the 1980s, Premier Zhao Ziyang declared his support for industrial policy, and took the first steps to creating industrial policy divisions within the existing planning bodies. Zhao argued that in China's immature market conditions of the 1980s, it was impossible to solely rely on market forces, and that industrial policy could serve to integrate the economic development strategy with economic system reform (Zhao 1987). This is an attractive concept, but China in practice never came close to realizing it.

In science and technology policy, new forms of government support developed during the 1980s with a dramatic burst of *consultation,* and then gradually coalesced into a more institutionalized system with greater division of labor and more clearly specified objectives. In 1986, a series of meetings between top politicians and scientists (triggered by a March letter from prominent scientists to Deng Xiaoping) quickly led to a new policy framework: a Science and Technology Leadership Small Group was established for coordination; the China National Natural Science Foundation was set up to distribute billions of RMB in grant money; and the 863 Plan was drafted to guide research priorities (Yu 2014). External evaluation of funding proposals was established, and the share of grants awarded by competitive evaluation increased through the 1990s. Still this program was primarily an enhancement of budgetary procedures, designed to distribute research funds more efficiently and to a broader range of clients. Moreover, the amounts were small well into the next century.

Interesting ideas were put forward, and the attraction of Japanese industrial policy is undeniable. Yet, by unanimous agreement, such efforts never really gained traction. Heilmann and Shih, in their penetrating discussion of industrial policy in China, attribute the failure during this period to the lack of "crucial institutional prerequisites, instruments, and bodies for implementing such policies" (Heilmann and Shih 2013:10). This is certainly true, but it must also be noted that the inconsistency of overall macroeconomic policy by itself made it impossible to lay out a coherent industrial policy. By trying to formulate and implement an industrial policy in a rapidly changing environment without adequate skills or instruments, industrial policy-makers were doomed to fail.

2.3. Waves of "Enlivening"

If industrial policy and planning did not steer the economy, what did? The answer is straightforward: market-oriented economic reforms are what actually shaped development. China followed a gradualist approach to economic reform and was careful to avoid the disruption and instability potentially caused by a "big bang." Inevitably, this implied that the implementation of reforms was uneven, coming at different times in different sectors. Generally, the sector with the biggest problems and the lowest profitability demanded reforms —something had to be done— and these reforms, after a lag, were generally successful in resolving the initial critical problems. In this way, successive waves of sector-focused reforms led to a pattern of other waves of "enlivening" and growth, of which it is straightforward to identify seven. These "waves" were the most important policy-induced forces shaping the composition (and thus ultimately the speed) of growth.

The first great enlivening took place in the farm economy from 1979 through 1983.[3] In the first step, constraints on farmers were relaxed beginning on what is, by convention, the very first day of the reform era. When the communique of the Third Plenum of the Eleventh Central Committee was published in December 1978,

3 This section draws on Naughton (2019).

it called for giving agriculture a chance to "catch its breath." This vague promise was quickly made good as policy-makers eased off on agricultural procurement quotas and provided better prices to farmers for their output. Note that this step took place at exactly the same time that policy-makers were abandoning the grandiose Ten-Year Plan. Indeed, the resources released by abandoning the plan were immediately made available for the relaxation of agricultural procurement policy (including through the expanded import of food grains). The liberalization of farm policy was a major policy shift, but it was not until the grant of land to the farmers, spreading nationwide between 1980 and 1982, that the farm economy was really enlivened. With various systems of contracting land to rural households, farmers were given the freedom to decide what to farm, when to farm, and when not to farm. The results are, of course, known to everyone: the farmers who had struggled to feed China for the previous twenty years, left to themselves, quickly produced surpluses that have been more than enough to provide abundance and diversity to China's mass middle-class society (Lin 1992). The relaxation of food constraints, in turn, gave policy-makers much greater room for maneuver, economically and politically, and set the stage for future waves of reform.

In parallel with the transformation of the agricultural economy, but logically dependent upon it for success, was the liberalization of the rural nonagricultural economy. This was the second great wave of enlivening. Left to their own devices, farmers found they could squeeze out a portion of household labor for nonagricultural tasks. Once farmers and villages were allowed to set up businesses, and send out salesmen and purchasing agents to support those businesses, a new explosion of labor-intensive manufactures emerged from the Chinese countryside. These new producers dramatically transformed the availability of simple but diverse products that broke the bleak monotony of consumer-goods supply under the bureaucratic economy. In addition, these new "township and village enterprises" (TVEs) provided competition for the state-owned enterprises (SOEs) that had been exploiting their monopoly position in industrial-product markets since the 1950s.

As policy-makers absorbed the lessons of the rural transformation, they began to allow a parallel relaxation in the urban economy. Cities were enlivened first by an explosion of small-scale private businesses that transformed services, retail, restaurants, and then small-scale industry. It took the personal approval of Deng Xiaoping to allow a seller of dried melon seeds from Anhui (*Shazi Guazi*) to expand a private business beyond household scale. Spanning a decade from about 1983 through 1993, China's cityscapes came alive. Indeed, the "internal opening" of Beijing to small-scale retail business after 1993 was one of the quickest signals that China had resumed liberalization after the post-Tiananmen reform rollback. To be sure, there was at this time no protection for the property rights of private corporations, but when the dams were torn down, there was an enormous reservoir of pent-up labor and entrepreneurship ready to step in and make China's small-scale sector an important contributor to growth and prosperity.

After the initial three waves of enlivening had taken place, Chinese policy-makers developed the will to engage the "hard core" of the socialist economy, large-scale state industry. These big SOEs were floundering during the 1990s, due to the enhanced competition from TVEs and private firms. Their situation was increasingly critical, as the net profit (after deducting losses) of all industrial SOEs declined, essentially to zero, in 1997. Yet the flip side of the impending bankruptcy of the SOEs was the fact that alternate businesses and ownership forms had reached sufficient scale to absorb the workers, land, and disused structures shed by bankrupt or collapsing SOEs. Moreover, an intensive effort to build fiscal, taxation, banking, and regulatory institutions appropriate to a market economy—sketched out in the 1993 Third Plenum (of the Fourteenth Central Committee)— achieved substantial success during the mid-1990s, sufficient to guide a profound institutional restructuring. As a result, it was possible to enliven the large-scale industrial sector by subjecting the state-owned enterprises to the nearly full brunt of competitive pressures for the first time in their history.

Self-evidently, the restructuring of state-owned industry was not the simple happy story of enlivening like the one that took place in the rural and private sectors. During a drastic and painful period from about 1996 to 2002, the state enterprise work force shrank by more than 40 percent, and the majority of smaller industrial SOEs went out of business. Many laid-off workers were unemployed for years before being either gradually absorbed back into the labor force at lower wages and status or accepting early retirement and withdrawing from the formal labor force. Despite this mid-term pain, the SOE reforms were in the end a story of enlivening as well. The remaining SOEs were substantially restructured around the turn of the century, often remade into joint-stock corporations, and most survived and returned to profitability.

As the earliest enlivening measures were running out of steam, and as the state sector was absorbing the shock to which it had been subjected, the greatest enlivening of all was finally building strength. Beginning in the 1990s, but accelerating steadily into the 2005–2010 period, the barriers between urban and rural were finally torn down, and 200 million migrants flooded into the urban economy. This fifth wave of enlivening gave an entirely new scale to the Chinese economy. The "floating population" —individuals away from their place of permanent household registration for more than six months— increased from almost nothing in 1990 to a peak of 253 million in 2014. These workers, literate, ambitious, equipped with cell phones and the will to build a new, modern China, were the key driver of growth acceleration in the twenty-first century. The gradual lowering of barriers to movement allowed under-employed rural young people to find new jobs and roles in the urban economy. As their potential productivity was brought into play, economic growth remained robust and even accelerated.

Even with rural China on the move, the potential of enlivening was not exhausted. Two more waves loomed, both of which were generally unanticipated consequences of decisions made during the accelerated reform period in the late 1990s. The sixth wave arose because of the decision made in 1998 to privatize urban housing. This decision was itself an offshoot of the great SOE reform and downsizing carried out at this time. In order to allow SOEs to go under without taking workers' living spaces with them, Premier Zhu Rongji agreed to a relatively comprehensive program of low-cost privatization of existing residential property. Most urban housing at that time was owned by the work unit, and each apartment built by the work unit now passed into the hands of the workers and staff who lived there. This simple decision triggered off the great Chinese housing boom that accelerated after about 2003. As Chinese households realized they had a valuable and appreciating asset that could be swapped for other, even nicer assets, with even greater appreciation potential, a new wave of upgrading and real estate speculation began. This became another of the great drivers of Chinese growth in the twenty-first century.

Finally, the decision to enter the World Trade Organization (WTO) touched off the seventh, export-oriented, wave of enlivening. As was the case with the housing market, there was a significant lag between the time the nominal decision was made and the time the response to that decision became manifest. China's WTO entry was agreed in 1999, but membership did not become final until December 2001, and even then, some of the most important provisions phased in over the next three years. As the new rules kicked in, as new producers and merchants entered while old ones learned new tricks, and as clumsy old businesses were forced out of the way, China's exports began to accelerate. Between 2004 and 2007, China's exports grew more than 30 percent per year, as new players found new markets. The enlivening of China's export economy was the seventh wave, the last in a series of enlivening reforms that released structural potential that had previously been suppressed.

2.4. The New Normal: Policy-Making Under Zhu Rongji

As described earlier, by the mid-1990s, disillusionment with planning and the success of market reforms meant that government intervention in sectoral development policy declined steadily. Such interventions reached a minimum during the Premiership of Zhu Rongji (1998-2003), when they were almost zero. On one side, technology policy became largely de-coupled from industrial policy, and instead became an almost purely "horizontal" policy for building human resources. Under the policy labeled "Revitalize the Nation through Science and Education [*kejiao xingguo*]," budgetary allocations for the Chinese Academy of Sciences increased, while competitive research grants through the National Natural Science Foundation of China expanded dramatically. The May 1998 "985 Program" increased funding for elite universities, and overall university enrollments began the rapid acceleration that would increase the number of college graduates from one million in 2001 to five million by 2007. Inputs into science, technology and innovation increased as budgetary resources became available.

In the industrial sector itself, Zhu Rongji abolished most of the industrial ministries in 1988, and converted that 242 national research institutes that had been affiliated with industrial ministries into independent enterprises. At the same time, during Zhu's premiership, the central government scaled down the large state-owned industrial projects that were intended to absorb advanced technology and reshape sectoral technology trajectories. This is evident in all three of the flagship high-tech investment projects: integrated circuit (IC) fabrication; nuclear power technology; and civilian aircraft. The 1995 government investment in IC fabrication, a joint venture with the Japanese firm NEC, was the last large-scale central government investment in IC production for over a decade. The project, as implemented under the Zhu administration, was not an abject failure, but was plagued by delays and cost overruns, and no successor project was initiated. In nuclear power, two large-scale projects had been ongoing since the 1980s, a domestically developed project (Qinshan) and a French turnkey project (Daya Bay near Hong Kong), both of which involved substantial investment in expanding domestic technological capabilities. Zhu did not approve any additional nuclear power plants during his administration. Finally, large civilian aircraft projects had been undertaken since the 1970s in a series of stop-and-go initiatives, with frequently shifting strategies. After the breakdown of cooperation with foreign partners in 1997-98, Zhu Rongji declined to resume independent efforts, and there was no large aircraft project for the remainder of his term.[4]

To be sure, the Chinese never adopted a laissez-faire philosophy towards technology, but practically speaking, the Chinese government by 2001 had stopped trying to enact specific industrial and technology outcomes. Industrial policies were maintained for a handful of the highest priority sectors, such as ICs, software, and automobiles, but the approach shifted to a relatively "light touch" policy, relying overwhelmingly on indirect instruments. The main industrial policy support for ICs and software was Document No. 18 of 2000, which threw the sector open to private and foreign investment, and which provided tax incentives to producers regardless of their ownership status.[5] China supported several industrial standards designed to benefit local firms, the most important of which was the TD-SCDMA third generation telecom standard (Linden 2004). No other sectors received anything like the level of attention given to ICs and telecom. Thus, by the end of the Zhu Rongji administration in 1998-2003, the government had wound down old-style government investment in state-owned techno-industrial projects, and had committed to a new, market-driven process.

Moreover, Zhu presided over an extensive government re-organization, specifically designed to reduce the amount of government oversight and control of firms, in order to make enterprises

4 For further documentation, see Chen and Naughton (2016).

5 IC industrial policy has been well covered in the literature. See Yinug (2009). Policies were further scaled back in 2004 to conform with WTO rules on tax rebates.

more fully market-oriented. Most industrial ministries were abolished, and the total personnel of the comprehensive economic agencies was reduced by 41% from 1,768 to 1,040. The authority to "draw up and implement industrial policy" was explicitly taken away from the State Planning Commission and given to the State Economic and Trade Commission, which did not have the institutional structures to formulate industrial policy, and in fact never did so (Jung 2008). In other words, there literally was no government agency taking charge of industrial policy. As Heilmann and Melton (2013) describe, while "planning" was still practiced, it was re-defined to produce a long-term strategic vision, without any imperative economic targets (Heilmann and Melton 2013:620-639). The 11th five-year plan (2006-2010) still fit in with this evolution. It laid out a development strategy rather than a bundle of industrial policies. It envisioned a broader and more environmentally-friendly development strategy, based on human capital development, poverty alleviation, and growth of the middle class (Naughton 2005). The 11th Plan thus represented the culmination of an evolution toward a more market-driven process, in which government largely withdraws from direct intervention and "vertical" policy-making.

The driving force of industrial development in Zhu's administration was market-oriented economic reform. Zhu took the difficult step of closing down under-performing state enterprises and further opening China's economy, a process that culminated in China's 2001 entry into the World Trade Organization (WTO). The de-emphasis and virtual abolition of targeted industrial interventions was a conscious and intentional part of this process, as can be seen from the fact that the organizational structures that organize policy-making were re-shaped to the type of market-friendly outcomes considered rational by the Zhu Rongji administration. This policy evolution at first seemed destined to continue under the new leadership post-2003, as exemplified by the new Premier Wen Jiabao. It seemed probable that technology and innovation policy would continue to evolve in the direction of market guidance. The expectation of continuity was reinforced by China's economic success, and deep integration into global production and technology networks. There had been fears in China of a painful economic consolidation in the wake of China's 2001 WTO membership. Instead, China's GDP growth *accelerated,* and stayed above 10% for five years beginning in 2003. Incoming foreign investment increased, for example in the semiconductor industry, where eight new plants were on the line and another 13 under construction by 2003, all foreign-invested or private (Chen 2011). Chinese firms were forced to upgrade to meet the intense competition, while the new foreign-invested firms had to localize activities and transfer technology to Chinese partners in order to be cost competitive. Both processes were effective in compelling technology adoption and improved productivity (Brandt, Van Biesenbroeck and Zhang 2012). China's integration into global production networks deepened, and China became the world's largest exporter of high-tech products (surpassing the US in 2005), with 88% of those exports produced by foreign-invested firms. China's success was especially marked in information and communications hardware (ICT), which offered relatively low-technology and low-capital intensity entry points, and also multiple pathways for upgrading to higher valued hardware, software, and service activities. For all these reasons, most analysts expected continuity in China's movement towards more market-based instruments, and few anticipated major changes.

2.5. Conclusions

By 2005, the Chinese economy was unquestionably a success of a global and historic dimension. Not only was overall growth extraordinarily rapid, but it had been accompanied by all the hallmarks of a broad development process. Living standards had improved rapidly in both city and countryside, skill and education levels had jumped, and urbanization was proceeding rapidly. In the international dimension, China had progressed far beyond the initial, limited export promotion through special policies, and was now entering an era of deeper openness. The harmonization of domestic and international economic rules, symbolized by WTO membership, seemed to be well under way. Moreover, China was entering an explosive growth phase in which integration of Chinese workers and producers into global value chains was transforming the world economy.

How much of that success could be attributed to industrial policy and planning? The answer is simple: none. So long as we retain a relatively narrow definition of industrial policy, it is quite clear that China through 2005 had very little of it, and that what it had was rarely even implemented, much less in an effective way. It was not unreasonable to expect continuity. However, as we show in the next chapter, the reality was that China was now poised to make a fateful turn in policy direction.

3

The Turning Point: Reviving Industrial Policy, 2006-2013

China began a new central government industrial policy in 2006 (Chen and Naughton 2016).[1] The new policies began when the Medium and Long Term Program of Science and Technology (MLP) was adopted in 2006, which laid out a fifteen-year program from 2006 through 2020. The MLP was not in itself an industrial policy, but it contained within it seeds that would grow into a full-fledged industrial policy over the next several years. The program, for the first time, emphasized "indigenous innovation" and provided funding for sixteen Megaprojects. This program started small, but gradually gained momentum. Then, when the global financial crisis (GFC) hit at the end of 2008, funding was quickly stepped up. In the wake of the GFC-related stimulus spending, a new effort was made to organize and rationalize the industrial policy push. This effort was finalized by late 2010 with the rollout of the new Strategic Emerging Industry (SEI) program. After 2010, China was committed to a full panoply of industrial policies.

1 This chapter includes material from that article.

The policy orientation had changed enormously since the late 1990s and the days of Premier Zhu Rongji.

3.1. The Resumption of Industrial Policy in 2006

When China resumed industrial policy in 2006, the initial approach was cautious and incremental. Policy-makers pursued what we might call a "top and bottom" approach. That is, policy-makers produced a broad innovation policy framework (the top) and also a list of projects to be funded by the government (the bottom). The innovation policy framework was broad and fairly diffuse, and generally appeared to be consistent with a "horizontal" approach, in which emphasis was placed on strengthening the overall innovation environment, rather than any specific sector.[2] Enterprises were identified as the prime actors in innovation. The slogan of "indigenous innovation," which was introduced at this time, could also support multiple different interpretations. In fact, the 2006 MLP was somewhat schizophrenic: many passages can be read as endorsements for a strongly market-oriented approach, following on the market reform successes of the previous decade, but other passages signal the need for greater government intervention in specific technologies (and, by implication, industries).

The bulk of the document (22 out of 39 pages) is taken up by three separate but over-lapping lists of technologies, categorized into 68 priority sectors, 27 frontier fields and 18 basic research areas. Reform of the science and technology system and building China's national innovation system are described in only four pages; policies and government measures in six; and human resources in two. The Megaprojects —on which I focus below— take up only a single page. There are only three numerical targets in the available summary document: by 2020, R&D should be 2.5%

2 Initial outside accounts of the MLP were generally positive for this reason (Schwaag Serger and Breidne 2007; Cao, Suttmeier and Simon 2006).

of GDP; dependence on foreign technology should decline to 30%; and increased productivity should account for 60% of total growth. The plan itself, then, is not really operational; rather, it lays out principles that are intended to guide subsequent action. In this sense, it is typical of the top-level, programmatic documents that form the keystone of the structured policy process in the Chinese system. It is couched in generalities, and of course the subject of the document is "innovation and science," not industrial policy.

However, the MLP was immediately followed by an implementation document that linked specific objectives in the full detailed plan (not publicly available) to specific bureaucratic agencies. The State Council published a document that listed 99 policy initiatives, and designated a head agency for each (State Council 2006).[3] Most implementation responsibilities were given to the economic ministries, with the National Development and Reform Commission (NDRC) —the former Planning Commission— receiving 29, and the Ministry of Finance (MOF) with 25. The prominent role of economic ministries followed logically from the principle that enterprises were the primary actors in the innovation process, since only the economic ministries were in a position to directly influence enterprise behavior. This document clearly implied that the strategy was a "full court press," that is, that a full spectrum of policy instruments should be applied to support innovation. For example, financial resources included direct government funding, subsidized lending, more-than-100% tax credits for R&D outlays, and so forth: an economic ministry or state bank would have to take the lead in each of these. This allocation of responsibilities brought the economic ministries back into direct industrial policies in a big way. The "hand off" of policy from the top leaders to the ministries gave much greater prominence to actors with stronger economic interests, and created a structure of expertise that was heavier on economic than on technological issues.

3 A subsequent retrospective study classified implementation actions into 65 "major" supporting policies and found that the Ministry of Finance was responsible for 22 of these (Ministry of Science and Technology Policy Regulation and System Reform Section 2007).

In fact, the incremental approach adopted was consistent with traditional Chinese approaches toward experimental policy-making. In a low-information environment, policy-makers started out by addressing and implicitly answering a few simple questions: Where are we going? What are the few essential things we should get started on? The first question pointed toward a broad re-orientation of economic policy toward support for innovation and more sophisticated sectoral structure of output. These things were essential, but also naturally-occurring; changes that would take place at the end of China's very high growth period, already looming. "Indigenous innovation" was part of this re-orientation, even if policy-makers were uncertain how to achieve this. The second question pointed to short-term support for a number of technological and industrial initiatives that would aid that transition. These were not very well specified, but the new policies clearly gave economic agencies permission to undertake a number of direct interventions to foster this type of technological innovation. The most immediately actionable of these interventions were the "Megaprojects."

3.2. The Megaprojects

Sixteen Megaprojects were mapped out in the wake of the MLP. Each of the Megaprojects was state-funded, but with an industrial policy objective. Megaprojects were expected to break bottlenecks and contribute to the development of a competitive industry, building innovative capabilities in sectors with a major impact on economic and social development. Most strikingly, the Megaprojects included IC fabrication, nuclear reactors, and large civilian airliner projects; each of the three areas terminated by the Zhu Rongji administration was brought back to life, bigger and with more resources than ever before.

For the 13 publicly known Megaprojects, the State Council was at the top of the hierarchy and the State S&T and Education Leadership Small Group, chaired by Premier Wen Jiabao, was in charge of overall coordination and guidance. The Ministry of Science and Technology (MOST) was the overall lead agency for the Megaprojects. The National Megaproject Office is physically located within MOST to organize the daily operations of the 10 civilian Megaprojects. However, with only 5 employees in its Megaprojects office, MOST primarily played a coordination role and shared information. At the ministry level, responsibilities include plan validation, coordination, evaluation, and reporting; here the Megaproject office is the mid-level decision maker and facilitator of communication.

At the project level, each Megaproject has a central ministry in charge of general management. For example, the pharmaceutical Megaproject is led by the Ministry of Health; the water pollution and prevention Megaproject is led by the Department of Environmental Protection. Each Megaproject also has a leading group, which includes a director, a (vice) minister, or a (deputy) director from MOST, MIIT, or another government entity. The leading groups' responsibilities are to organize and coordinate the operations of each Megaproject. This includes recruiting a project chief designer (an engineer), organizing the formulation of plans, arranging applications for subprojects, selecting the advisory board, and appointing a supervisory board. As a whole, the Megaprojects reflect a top-down approach, nominally centralized, where decisions flow hierarchically. Each Megaproject was structured to reflect its own unique characteristics: at one extreme, the space program is a single massive integrated program; at the other, the "core electronic components" program was essentially a coordinated funding agency, with many different research projects contracted out to domestic companies and research institutes. Management of individual Megaprojects was parceled out among 12 different ministries, including the military, plus 2 provinces, 3 state-owned enterprises, and one university (full list below in Table 3.1). Typically, a separate ministry was given oversight responsibilities for each Megaproject. Policy specification continued until the complex structure of each Megaproject was agreed upon and approved, and work began. The first completely new Megaproject was approved in April 2008 with the launch of the core electronic components project, and the last approval came in May 2010 for the high resolution earth observation satellite.

3.2.1. Technology Choice in the Megaprojects

For the most part, the MLP Megaprojects are large-scale goal-driven projects focusing on the advancement of engineering rather than basic science capabilities. They are clearly influenced by "industrial policy" considerations, in that the selection of civilian projects is obviously influenced by a view as to which industries are relatively promising. However, they are not directly industrial policies themselves since they do nothing to direct resources to specific industrial sectors. How the technologies are to be transferred to businesses remains unspecified.

The MLP groups together nine civilian and seven military/dual-use Megaprojects, 13 of which are known to the public while three remain unpublished. However, according to various internet sources, the three defense Megaprojects have been deduced to be: the Shenguang Inertial Confined Fusion (ICF) Project; the Beidou Navigation System; and the Hypersonic Technology Vehicle. Of these, the Beidou system is viewed as a success and is now publicly acknowledged as a Megaproject, while information on the other projects is classified and extremely scarce. Table 3.1 illustrates the stated goals and level of funding (as of 2009-2010) of the technologies developed by the 16 Megaprojects.

Table 3.1: Overview of the 16 MLP Megaprojects

Project Name	Sector	Project Goals	Total Funding (in RMB)
Core electronics, high-end general microchips, and basic software	Civilian	Develop high-end communication microchips, basic software, and core electronic components	100 billion (estimated)

ULSI manufacturing technology	Civilian	Industrialize the 90 nm ULSI, produce sample machinery for the 60nm ULSI and acquire key technologies in making the 45 nm ULSI	18 billion
Next generation broadband wireless mobile communication	Civilian	1. Upgrade technologies of the current cellular mobile communication system, including high-speed packet access (HSPA), i.e., 4G; 2. Develop Broadband wireless access technology, including WiMax; 3. Develop a short-distance wireless system and censor network	70 billion (20b from central government)
High-end CNC machine tools and basic manufacturing technology	Civilian	Improve China's manufacturing abilities of high-end machinery: e.g., high-precision machinery for aviation, space, shipbuilding, and other industries	21 billion
Large-layer oil and gas fields and coal-bed methane development	Civilian	Develop exploration and mining technologies for oil, gas, and coal-bed methane resources under complex geological conditions in Western China	60 billion (20b from central government)
Large-scale advanced pressurized water reactor (PWR) nuclear power plant and high temperature reactor (HTR)	Dual-use	Obtain key technologies in PWR and build the first commercial plant; acquire key technologies and build a demonstration plant using HTR	15 billion from central government (11.92b to PWR; 3b to HTR)

Water pollution control and treatment	Civilian	Control and protect pollution, develop water treatment technologies, support coordination of regional water access and ecological planning	30 billion (estimated)
Genetic transformation and breeding of new plants	Civilian	Research transgene technologies to develop new pest-resistant breeds of higher quality and productivity	20 billion
Research and creation of major new drugs for China	Civilian	Develop 30 to 40 drugs new to Chinese production with market competitiveness and intellectual property protection	55 billion (estimated)
Prevention and control of major infectious diseases, including HIV/AIDS and Viral Hepatitis	Civilian	Develop new vaccines and treatment methods for infectious diseases such as HIV/AIDS and Viral Hepatitis	Unknown
High-resolution Earth observation system	Dual-use	Develop an observation system consisting of satellites, aircraft, and stratospheric airships; build ground facilities such as observatories and data centers to enhance self-supply of spatial data	40 billion
Large passenger aircraft (C919)	Civilian	Design and build China's first large passenger aircraft C919	200 billion (estimated)
Manned space flight and lunar exploration	Dual-use	Implement the Chang'e lunar probe and Shenzhou manned spaceship	Shenzhou budget 39 billion until 2013
Shenguang Inertial Confined Fusion (ICF)	Defense	*Information not released*	Unknown

Beidou Navigation System	Defense	Build a navigation network consisting of 30 satellites by 2020 (S&T Daily 2012)	Unknown
Hypersonic Technology Vehicle	Defense	*Information not released*	Unknown

Sources: own elaboration. There are no comprehensive published accounts for the Megaprojects. The table was compiled from 2009-2010 press reports by Lu et. al (2012).

3.2.2. Megaproject Management

The Megaprojects were set up in a careful fashion, with a "dual leadership" system. A standard Megaproject has a leading group with a vice minister as the head and a working office located in one of its supervisory ministries. The research side is then organized with a chief engineer or designer and several deputy chief engineers. They serve the main role of planning and supervising the R&D activities. In addition to this "standard model," however, two Megaprojects were organized as corporations and given a more market-oriented perspective. These were the C919 Large Passenger Aircraft project and the large-scale advanced pressurized water reactor (PWR) nuclear power plant and high temperature reactor (HTR). The most distinctive feature of the large aircraft project is that an independent company, Commercial Aircraft Corporation of China, Ltd. (COMAC), was created to run the Megaproject as a business rather than a government project. China National Nuclear Power Cooperation (CNPTC) was established, as a state-owned enterprise (SOE) owned solely by the state. In a significant innovation, COMAC was set up as a joint stock corporation; its shareholders include SASAC, Shanghai Guosheng Group Corporation (founded by the Shanghai government), Aviation Industry Corporation of China (AVIC), China Aluminum Corporation (CHINALCO), and other SOEs. As the Shanghai government is COMAC's second largest shareholder, this indicates that, of all the provinces bidding for C919, Shanghai gained the most in the competition for C919 stock.

Both of these corporations were established to meet two objectives: on the one hand, they were designed to give participants a clearer market goal than was the case for the other Megaprojects; on the other hand, they were established in part to resolve conflicts and lobbying among existing stake-holders and localities. By requiring "buy in" from these competing stake-holders (literally so, in the case of COMAC), the corporation became a form for regulating competing interests. In some important respects, the COMAC model was a precursor of approaches that became much more common over the next 15 years. As chapter 5 will demonstrate, joint ownership by diverse state-controlled entities is now a common form of organizing industrial policy initiatives.

The Megaprojects are said to be supervised by an evaluation system operated jointly by MOST, NDRC and MOF. The supervision mainly focuses on two aspects: project implementation and financial management. Four supervisory groups were formed in 2010 and 2011 to perform evaluation work: the electronic and information technology group, energy and environment protection group, biology and pharmaceutics group and advanced manufacturing group. The evaluation system for the military and dual-use Megaprojects remains unknown, and internal auditing, inspection and evaluation processes remain opaque.

3.2.3. Evolution of the Megaprojects

The Megaprojects were all set up in 2007 and 2008, but spending began in 2008. However, total outlays were just 6 billion RMB, as several of the Megaprojects were still in preliminary organization. When the global financial crisis (GFC) hit at the end of 2008, the Chinese government responded with a massive stimulus effort. As part of that response, Megaproject implementation was accelerated, and an attempt was made to hurry all projects into implementation by the end of 2009 (Chen 2010). Disbursements spiked to 33 billion RMB in 2009, and then resumed more normal growth, leveling off at around 45-50 RMB annually. While small in relation to today's industrial policy effort, these sums meant that the Chinese government was now sustaining a significant flow of resources into the industrial policy arena.

3.3. The Second Wave: Strategic Emerging Industries

The strategic emerging industries (SEI) program constituted a second wave of techno-industrial policy. There are both similarities and important differences between the Megaprojects and the SEIs. There is significant sectoral overlap: some SEI initiatives are direct continuations of individual Megaprojects, and most Megaprojects have some relation with a subsequent SEI. Since the Megaprojects were from the start directed at technologies that could be quickly commercialized, and given that there are many more SEIs than Megaprojects, this relationship is to be expected (see Table 3.2 for full list).

3.3.1. A Fully-Fledged Industrial Policy

The most important distinction between the SEI program and the existing Megaprojects was that the SEI program was from the beginning an industrial policy. Unlike the Megaprojects, which are fully government funded, SEI development is not to be driven *primarily* by government funding. Instead, government is supposed to "make the market," creating favorable conditions for enterprises to develop and grow. The lead agency for SEIs was always the NDRC, the main economic planning agency, in contrast to the MLP and Megaprojects which were initially led by MOST and started as science policy, and only subsequently spilled over into industrial policy. The SEI program sets specific goals, roadmaps, and targets for all its designated industries. In this sense, the SEIs are best thought of as a continuation of the "full court press" that emerged from the specification of MLP policies by the economic ministries.

The preferential policies are more sharply focused on specific sectors, and this naturally establishes substantial continuity with the Megaprojects (Table 3.2).

Table 3.2: Sectorial Targets of Industrial Policy

	16 Megaprojects (2006-2015)			20 Strategic Emerging Industries (2010-2020)
				Energy Conservation and Environmental Protection
			a.	Energy efficient machinery
1	1 Water pollution control and treatment	→	b.	Environmental protection
			c.	Recycling and Re-utilization
2	ULSI Semiconductor Manufacturing			**Next Generation Information Technology**
3	Next generation broadbrand wireless	→	d.	Next generation internet
4	Core electronics and high end software	→	e.	Core electronic components
		↘	f.	High end software and information services
				Biotechnology
5	Mayor New Drug Initiative	→	g.	Biopharmaceuticals
6	Major Infection Desease Initiative		h.	Biomedical engineering
7	Genetic transformation and plant breeding	→	i.	Biological Agriculture
			j.	Bio-manufacturing Industry
				Precision and High-End Machinery
8	Large Passenger Aircraft	→	k.	Commercial Aircraft
9	High-Resolution Earth Observation System	→	l.	Satellites and Applications
10	Manned Space Flight and Lunar Landing	↗	m.	Railroad and Transport Machinery
			n.	Marine Engineering Equipment
11	High-end Numerically Controlled Machine Tools		o.	Intelligent Manufacturing Equipment

			New Energy
12	Large-bed Oil & Gas; Coal Gasification	p.	Wind Power
13	Large High-Pressure Nuclear Reactor Technology	q.	Solar Power
		r.	Biomass Energy
14-16	Three Undiscloser Military Projects		**New Materials**
		s.	New Materials
			New Energy Vehicles
		t.	Electric Vehicles & Plug-in Hybrids

Sources: own elaboration based on Chen and Naughton (2016).

Sectors are included in the SEI initiative because they are expected to be large and important in the future, but also because they have qualitatively new elements that have not been fully mastered anywhere in the world. Because of the absence of entrenched incumbent firms or countries, these industries are seen as providing competitive opportunities. SEI strategy thus reflects the insight that new industries present an opportunity for leapfrog latecomer development (Perez and Soete 1988). The SEI program reflects an attention to a high degree of technological opportunity, combined with confidence that the returns on innovation will be appropriable, given China's ongoing manufacturing cost advantages. The SEI approach is encapsulated in the often-repeated slogan: "seize the commanding heights of the new technological revolution" (Wan 2009).

3.3.2. Formulation of the SEIs

The SEI program came together quickly in the wake of the Global Financial Crisis (GFC), whose shockwave hit China in late 2008. As is known, China's response to the GFC was large, prompt, and decisive: A large fiscal stimulus was quickly followed by a massive flood of bank credit. The initial response relied primarily on "horizontal" fiscal and monetary policies to pump up domestic demand to offset the impact of rapidly falling exports. However, government quickly followed up with interventions into specific industrial sectors, beginning with those severely crisis-hit. A package of ten "Industrial Revitalization" policies was rolled out in February 2009 covering ten mostly traditional industries (steel, autos, etc.), which though highly interventionist, were potentially short-term crisis responses. In fact, central government support expanded rapidly into high technology industries, while local governments began to convert the financial windfall from the stimulus into longer-term industrial development programs.[4]

The concept of "strategic emerging industries" sprung from this environment of rapid-fire pragmatic intervention (Zheng 2010). Fermentation occurred as policy-makers and intellectuals cast around for a rationale to convert ad hoc interventions into a long-turn program. Premier Wen Jiabao played a prominent role from the beginning, so fermentation led briskly into policy formulation. In the fall, Wen presided over a series of brainstorming sessions on the impact of new technologies, involving 47 scientists, engineers, and entrepreneurs. Ultimately, Wen found a sweeping justification for a major initiative: According to Wen, all through history, major crises like the GFC were followed by major technological breakthroughs. The countries that mastered these revolutionary new technologies transformed their economies and became the successful (and dominant) economies of the post-crisis eras. Developed countries were redoubling their support for emerging industries to mitigate crisis, and China should seize this opportunity. Wen poignantly contrasted the present opportunity with four instances since the 1700s when, he said, China had missed a technological revolution, and fallen behind as a result.

In November 2009, Wen Jiabao formally announced a Strategic Emerging Industries initiative, and selected seven broad industrial sectors for inclusion; the top leadership collectively endorsed the policy the next month at the Economic Work Conference. The

4 For example, see the two successive State Council documents (2009/a/b).

cornerstone of the policy formulation process was laid early the following year, when an Inter-ministerial Coordinating Group on Accelerating the Development of the SEIs was constituted. Made up of representatives from 20 ministries and chaired by the NDRC, the group held its first meeting on February 7, 2010. Its goal was to write a programmatic SEI policy, which would lead into an SEI Five Year Plan for the 12th Plan Period (2011-2015). A writing group under the Coordination Group was set up, again headed by the NDRC (a vice-minister, Zhang Xiaoqiang). Besides coordinating divergent ministerial interests, the group established a robust consultation process. During March and April 2010, a series of local studies and meetings were held in Wuhan, Shenyang, and Shenzhen involving state enterprises and a few well-established private firms. Studies were commissioned from the Chinese Academies of Science and Engineering and compiled with comparative international data into a 3,000-page collection of reference materials.

Given the high level of agreement that had already been established on an SEI policy, policy formulation largely focused on the scope of the program. After occasionally contentious discussions, Wen Jiabao's original seven broad sectors were augmented with the addition of "precision and high-end machinery" as a major sector (Table 3.2); while "new drugs" and "genetically-modified organisms" were consolidated into a "biotechnology industry," maintaining seven total sectors. "Electric vehicles" was replaced with the more cautious "new energy vehicles" (including hybrids). These changes made the SEIs much larger and shifted the definition further from a technology focus to an industrial policy focus. The addition of "high-end equipment manufacturing" included large machine-building sectors that were certainly not "new" or "emerging," globally or within China. These changes reflected the procedural influence exercised by the lead economic planning agency.

The State Council passed the keystone SEI document, "Decision to Accelerate the Cultivation of Strategic Emerging Industries" on October 10, 2010 (State Council 2010). This was good timing. A week later, the 5th Plenum of the Communist Party Central

Committee passed the "Party Center Suggestions on drawing up the 12th Five-Year Plan for National Social and Economic Development" (CCP 2010), which was the keystone document for the five year planning process. The SEI processes and the Five Year Plan processes were now fully in step. From a situation a decade earlier in which Five Year Plans had become almost irrelevant, the coordination of SEIs and the 12th Five Year Plan had now brought this plan back toward the center of economic policy-making.

The policy specification stage now proceeded in tandem for the SEIs and the 12th Five Year Plan (12FYP). Responsibility for drawing up a sector-specific 12FYP was delegated to a ministry or subministry. Overall specification was handled "in house" by the Inter-Ministerial Coordination Group, and again specific policy responsibilities were disaggregated to ministries. All the main government financing agencies and regulatory bodies signed memoranda of participation in a joint financing program, utilizing loans, stock markets, bond issuance, and increased investment funds, including venture funds. Direct funding from the government budget was to account for only 5-15% of the total funding effort (Fang and Yang 2011). In short, while the Megaprojects were directly funded by the government, the SEIs were to rely on indirect support from the government, through (government-owned) financial institutions, tax exemptions, and regulatory support.

Two dozen sector-specific 12-FYPs, each covering a single SEI, were issued in 2012. While the planning process had been top-down until this point, and from general to specific, the original SEI drafting group now stepped in for a second round, aggregating the individual sectoral plans into a "portmanteau" document that covered the entire SEI program. This document was submitted to the State Council, which approved it and formally issued it on July 9, 2012. This completed the policy specification process, as all tasks had been turned over to the implementing bodies, and the SEI program became a solidly entrenched part of the Chinese policy regime. It has remained so today, although, as the next chapter shows, it underwent significant revisions in 2015-2016.

3.4. SEIs and the Policy Turning Point

Implementation of the SEI policy is a work in progress. Since 2009, policy has been adapted to changing circumstances in a broad range of diverse sectors. As was the case with the Megaprojects, multiple and overlapping instruments are used in SEI implementation, and local and central government agencies cooperate and compete in the promotion of SEIs and support for specific firms. From the beginning of January 2011 through June 2014, the State Council and various national ministries promulgated 439 different policies to implement the SEIs (China Engineering Technology Development Strategy Academy 2015). Local governments have plunged into the implementation of the SEI program. Due to the proliferation of instruments, it is impossible to estimate the overall resource effort involved in the SEI program. However, it is clear that this effort grew dramatically in the years after the GFC in 2008. The magnitude of the program has been consolidated and expanded steadily in the decade since.

The dramatic change of policy is indicated by the pervasiveness of the new policy guidelines. Back in 2000, the government's guiding policy principle had been that market forces would drive decision-making, and that these forces would ultimately determine the sectoral development of the economy. By 2010, the guiding policy principle was that sectoral priorities outlined in the SEIs would guide government decision-making at all levels, and that governments would guide firms to follow in these directions. Not only were the big ticket items eliminated under Zhu Rongji brought back (as Megaprojects), but the direction of change and the principles on which policy was based were both reversed. Moreover, close analysis of the policy process shows that the apparent "over-shooting" of policy (compared to the vague language of the apex document) was actually an intrinsic feature of the procedures through which policy was specified and implemented.

Finally, the fact that two successive structured processes of policy change succeeded one another in a short time helps explain how policy could have changed so dramatically. The MLP was a major change of direction, but initially a rather modest resource commitment to the new policy direction. But just at the moment when the MLP was going into full implementation, another wave of policy-making was triggered by the impact of the GFC. The response to the GFC greatly encouraged Chinese policy-makers. The massive Chinese stimulus program was generally welcomed and highly appraised in international opinion. Moreover, Chinese policy-makers did not fail to notice that developed market economies had resorted to direct government interventions —and in targeted industries— when they had to move decisively to stave off economic collapse. Post-crisis, China also had to move decisively, either to roll back stimulus measures as the economy recovered, or to package them and give them a deeper rationale. They chose the second, and before initial interventions could be assessed or re-evaluated, they were re-launched with even greater vigor, and with more generality and more specificity. Thus, at the end, the two waves of the MLP and SEIs were enough to launch China into a completely new industrial policy regime.

3.5. Conclusions

The Chinese approach to industrial policy made a 180 degree turn after 2006. How is it that such a dramatic change in policy attracted so little attention at the time? The answer lies in the distinction between policy innovation and resource allocation. The year 2006 was clearly a turning point in the sense of policy innovation. In contrast to the Zhu Rongji era, Premier Wen Jiabao signaled in 2006 his determination to have the central government directly shape the industrialization trajectory. Government investment, via the Megaprojects, and targeted subsidies quickly became a permanent part of the policy mix. Yet initially these interventions were minuscule in relation to the economy as a whole. "Indigenous innovation" attracted discussion and elicited debate around the world, but it was still seen as a relatively small part of Chinese development policy, and this was appropriate. Also, it took time to set up an administrative structure to administer these grants, to say nothing of a planning structure for making determinations about priorities.

The situation began to change as the world tipped into the Global Financial Crisis (GFC). The administrative structures to run the Megaprojects were put in place just before the GFC and as the GFC was starting. Ramping up of the Megaprojects thus took place in the context of the vast Chinese stimulus program of 2008-9. Chinese policy-makers declared at the beginning of this stimulus program that it would be focused on infrastructure and would in principle not direct stimulus funds to industry at all. Outside observers took note of these principles. But as the GFC worsened, governments everywhere increased their stimulus policies, including programs to support industry, both emerging sectors and hard-hit traditional industries. China was no different (as described in Chapter 3.3.2.), and the result was that aggregate resource flow into industrial policy soared. After the GFC, though, most developed market economies dialed back their stimulus efforts, including both their emergency aid to troubled companies and their support for promising technologies of the future. At this point, China went its own way. It consolidated its industrial policy initiatives, gave them a new rationale (strategic emerging industries), and made an unprecedented national commitment to running sectoral industrial policies. For China, this was the "lesson" of the GFC: robust and decisive government intervention could and should complement the market economy. Both the policy orientation and the resource commitment had by this time changed completely from what it had been a decade earlier.

4

The Innovation-Driven Development Strategy, 2015-Present

China launched a new wave of industrial policies in 2015-2016. The opening maneuvers in this new campaign were the important stand-alone plans, "Made in China 2025" and the "Internet Plus Program," both made public in 2015. Then, in May 2016, the government approved a new integrating vision, a kind of master plan, entitled the "Innovation-driven Development Strategy" (IDDS) (CCP Party Center and State Council 2016). At about the same time, the existing Strategic Emerging Industries (SEI) plan was reconfigured to make it more operational, coherent, and consistent with the IDDS. Thus, within a couple of years, China adopted a portfolio of industrial policies, tied together with a vision statement. This new wave of industrial policy was a new departure, because it was focused on an emerging technological revolution. It was also an acceleration of existing industrial policies, substantially stepping up the overall resource effort. The high-level policy commitment to the new strategy was accompanied by the launch of a new funding device, government industrial guidance funds.

The first section of this chapter looks at the technological orientation of the new cluster of policies. It is sometimes said that Chinese planners were shocked into recognizing the power and significance of artificial intelligence by the 2015-2016 games in which the AlphaGo Artificial Intelligence program triumphed over the world's top-ranked Go players. In this version of events, AlphaGo served as a kind of "Sputnik moment" for Chinese planners, many of whom consider the game of Go to be more complex and more subtle than chess, and were thus shocked that a program, designed in the West, could beat the world's best players.[1] The chronology shows that China was already ramping up new policies when the shock of AlphaGo occurred, but this event can still serve as a symbolic moment in the creation of a new policy package. Ultimately, it is the orientation toward an emerging technological revolution that most sharply distinguishes Chinese industrial policy today from all other cases of industrial policy. The following section sketches out the scale of resource effort in the new policies, arguing that the magnitude of the current wave is much larger than any precedents. The third section discusses the implied economic strategy of current policies. The two final sections consider the impact of 2020 "New Infrastructure" policies, and provide a preliminary economic evaluation.

4.1. Targeting a Technological Revolution

The technological conception behind the IDDS marks it off from earlier Chinese industrial policies (and indeed, from earlier industrial policy in Japan or Korea). As described in the preceding chapter, the initial drafts of industrial policy in 2006 targeted a limited range of technologies and laid out a fairly traditional agenda of industrial catch-up. The sixteen 2006 "megaprojects" were, generally speaking, straightforward attempts to replicate existing

1 The crucial event came in March 2016, when Korea's Lee Sedol, arguably the world number two player, lost 4 games to 1 to AlphaGo. AlphaGo was created by DeepMind, subsequently acquired by Google.

industrial capabilities in advanced economies. The large civilian airliner and the Beidou geographic positioning system are good examples. In this sense, the initial version of Chinese industrial policy was a reincarnation of the classic latecomer catch-up strategy. This approach has two obvious advantages. First, the technological solutions adopted in advanced economies can be copied, replicated, or, when necessary, worked around. There are a number of "latecomer advantages" that can possibly be exploited, ranging from the market for cheap knock-offs to incremental improvements. Most important, policy-makers have certainty that a certain type of production can be achieved, so risk is concentrated in a limited range of achievable cost and quality dimensions. Second, industrial policy-makers can use the developmental trajectories of advanced economies to identify industries that are ripe for promotion. Japan's MITI famously targeted industrial sectors where the income elasticity in the middle income range was greater than one, including automobiles and chemicals. The (correct) assumption was that Japan would replicate the structural transformations of early developers.

The SEIs began the break with a traditional approach. The entire conception of "Strategic Emerging Industries" as elaborated in 2010 was that China could get in on the ground floor of entirely new industries in which there were no powerful entrenched incumbents. In 2010, Chinese policy-makers began to speak of "occupying the commanding heights of the technology revolution."[2] Individual sectors seemed to offer the potential not just to catch up, but to surpass the others. However, beyond this commonality of theme, the SEIs were a grab bag of sectors selected for hope-for breakout potential. There was no internal logic that tied individual sectors together; they included high-impact

2 This was in part due to the impact of the Global Financial Crisis (GFC). As part of their stimulus programs during the crisis, the advanced economies, including the U.S., targeted newly emerging industries, like solar energy, intelligent electric grid, and improved batteries. For Chinese policy-makers, this confirmed the potential significance of their long-sought goal of skipping stages and moving directly into new industries.

drugs and electric vehicles, along with mobile internet and oceanic machinery.

The IDDS, by contrast, is built around the idea that a very specific wave of technological change is beginning. The configuration of this wave of technological change thus gives increasingly a definite form to policy. It also means that, in the IDDS, the opportunity to move directly to the technological frontier and surpass other economies is no longer a wished-for feature of a few random sectors, but rather a fundamental feature of the current global moment. Increasingly, Chinese industrial policy is based on the idea that China has a once-in-a-lifetime opportunity to get in on the ground floor of a technological revolution and vault into the leading ranks of economic and technological powers. As the IDDS itself states:

> A new round of global technological revolution, sectoral change and military change is accelerating, and scientific exploration is unfolding at every scale from the microscopic to the cosmological. A group of revolutionary new technologies that are intelligent, green and ubiquitous are reshaping the global competitive landscape and changing the relative strength of nations (CCP Party Center and State Council 2016).

The changing "relative strength of nations" implies the opportunity to "surpass," as well as the danger of falling farther behind.

These technologies, jointly, are conceived of as a single "general purpose technology" that will be implemented across the board in society, improving productivity in many industrial sectors, as well as agriculture and services. These technologies are familiar to anyone who follows science and technology today. They are founded on the triangle of communication, data, and artificial intelligence. China is already by far the world's largest mobile internet market. Now the arrival of fifth generation (5G) communications technology provides enormous new capabilities for networked communication. To be sure, 5G is faster than 4G, making it more convenient and efficient. But even more important is the fact that 5G allows the seamless integration of local and global networks. This creates the opportunity for numerous local networks with a latency close-to-zero, which allows things like remote surgery in real time. These local networks are also critical for the development of driverless vehicles and truly intelligent traffic control networks. Data are increasingly being generated by massive networks of sensors of all kinds, from satellites to street cameras. As sensors proliferate, data proliferates at an exponentially greater rate, since each sensor creates an ongoing stream of data. Techniques to process data are improving by leaps and bounds, and artificial intelligence provides the opportunity not just to manage data, but also to derive higher level conclusions and interactions from patterns in the data. Together, the three clusters of communication, data and A.I. constitute a triangle of interacting capabilities that reinforce each other and create a single general purpose (GP) technology that has implications in every area of society and the economy.

Because of the emphasis on GP technologies and a coming technological revolution, IDDS is less specifically defined by individual industrial sectors than earlier waves of Chinese industrial policies. Progress in many sectors will contribute to the relative success of the IDDS, and overall progress will make success in individual sectors more likely. For example, more sophisticated robotics and smart networks will allow China's traditional industries to become more efficient, allowing them to retain competitiveness in an environment in which Chinese worker wages are rising rapidly. Alternately stated, the complementarity of many different sectors builds on China's strengths and gives China a unique opportunity. Section 4.6 provides further discussion of this strategy and the potential complementarity of different industries.

Despite this complementarity, IDDS retains the basic feature of previous industrial policies in that it explicitly targets a range of specific sectors and steps up the resource commitment to those sectors. In that sense, the *name* of the *innovation*-driven development strategy is rather misleading. Nearly every country has an innovation strategy, and almost everyone thinks innovation is a good thing, and therefore it might seem that China is simply doing what other countries do. For most countries, though, innovation strategy is predominantly a horizontal policy that aims at improving the environment for innovation and entrepreneurship in general, without targeting specific sectors. In fact, the components of IDDS make it clear that the definition of "innovation" in use corresponds to "technological upgrading." Josef Schumpeter long ago introduced the distinction between invention (a novel idea for how to do things) and innovation (carrying it out into practice). According to Edler and Fagerberg (2017:4) "what matters economically and societally is not the idea itself but its exploitation in the economic and social system… innovation is… the introduction of new solutions in response to problems or opportunities that arise in the social and/or economic environment?… in low-tech as well as high-tech."[3] By contrast, the official Chinese use of "innovation" almost always refers to "technological upgrading," in which highly qualified and credentialed personnel, working in sophisticated environments, are integrating more sophisticated procedures into the production process. Businesses that pioneer low-tech innovations, for example, bicycle-sharing (although that uses sophisticated internet-based interfaces) are not the focus of policy. While this is a broader, bolder, and more integrative industrial policy, it still relies primarily on the traditional industrial policy framework of industrial targeting.

4.2. A Key National Policy

The IDDS encompasses more sectors and more sectoral policies than China's previous industrial policies. Moreover, more attention is focused on the cross-sectoral impact of policies. As a result, the IDDS is expected to affect every aspect of society and the economy. This important feature is built into the policy design of the IDDS.

3 Edler and Fagerberg (2017) characterize innovation policies as mission-oriented, invention-oriented, or system-oriented. Chinese policies are a mix of all three.

4.2.1. A Portfolio of Policies with an Integrating Vision

The IDDS is an umbrella policy that includes many specific industrial policies as components. The "Industrial Policy Timeline" below shows both the "Made in China 2025" (State Council 2015/a; Wubbeke et. al 2015) and the "Internet Plus" (State Council 2015/b) policies preceding the IDDS, rolling out in 2015. Both these policies emphasize the application of new technologies to existing industrial sectors. "Made in China 2025" resembles Germany's "Industry 4.0" in its technological conception (though it is much larger in resource effort), calling for the integration of robotics, precision engineering, and ubiquitous sensors into "smart manufacturing" networks. These policies are highly actionable, and arguably represent a response to a new opportunity, that is, to introduce new general purpose technologies into traditional industries, where such technologies might not be well-known. The subsequent release, in May 2016, of the "Innovation-driven

Table 4.1: Industrial Policy Timeline

2005	11th Five Year Plan
2006	ML Term Science & Technology Plan
2010	Strategic Emerging Industries
2011	12th Five Year Plan
2015	Made in China 2025 Internet Plus
2016	IDDS National Plan SEIs 13th Five Year Plan
2017	Military-Civilian Fusion Plan Artificial Intelligence Plan AI 3-Year Action Plan
2018	Other 3-Year Action Plans Intelligent Photovoltaics; Intelligent Shipbuilding Cloud Computing; Information Consumption
2019	Internet and Services

Sources: own elaboration compiled by the author from data supplied by Zero2IPO / Qingke Research Center (清科研究中心). Accessed at https://www.pedata.cn/. Some data may be behind paywalls.

Development Strategy" (IDDS), was clearly an effort to integrate previously disparate strands of policy-making into an over-arching vision of technological change.

At the same time, the SEI program was revised to become a component of the broader IDDS. In November 2016, the Strategic Emerging Industries (SEI) Plan for the 13th FYP period (2016-2020) was issued. It contained broad targets for industrial sectors and dis-aggregated implementation tasks to numerous government agencies (State Council 2016).[4] Moreover, the new SEI plan called for close coordination with the slightly earlier Made in China 2025 and Internet Plus plans, as well as with the Military Civilian Industry Fusion Plan that followed shortly thereafter (Xia and Li 2016). Within the SEI plan, five large sectors were designated for immediate action, while four large sectors are designated for "preparatory work for later action." Each of what we might call the Big 5 has a target for output value in 2020: IT industry (12 trillion RMB); high-quality industrial equipment (12 trillion RMB); bio and pharmaceuticals (8-10 trillion); new energy vehicles and clean energy (10 trillion); and digital media (8 trillion). The four sectors being nurtured for later do not have output targets: they are Space and Ocean Exploration; information networks; life sciences; and nuclear technology. The plan also includes a number of sections on the creation of industrial clusters.

Between 2015 and 2017, then, policy-makers sought to integrate existing initiatives and produced a full panoply of interlocking plans. The IDDS sat at the apex, with at least five major programs under its broad umbrella. Four of these were targeted sectoral plans, and the fifth, the SEI itself encompassed a broad range of production sectors. Clearly, the span of industrial policy was substantially increased by this complex of policies.

4 The SEI plan for the previous five-year period, adopted July 9, 2012, can be accessed at http://www.gov.cn/zwgk/2012-07/20/content_2187770.html.

4.2.2. Authoritative National Policy

The IDDS is an unusually authoritative document. Because China has a hierarchical governmental system, the exact level of government that issues a policy is of great importance. If a ministry issues a document, for example, it is not binding on other ministries.[5] The IDDS is issued jointly by the Communist Party Center and the government State Council, giving it the highest possible political imprimatur: this document is binding on everybody in the political system. The IDDS is thus far more authoritative than policies that are issued by the State Council alone, or else drafted by Ministries and promulgated by the State Council Office. In addition, the IDDS is designed for the long term. It is formulated in "three stages": becoming an "innovative nation" by 2020; relying on innovation for economic growth and emerging as a leading innovative nation by 2030; and becoming a technological superpower by 2050. It is not clear that these stages have much concrete significance, but together they consolidate the expectation that this is a long-term strategy, not to be subject to the short-term whims of policy-makers. It is also not accidental that 2050 is one year after the one-hundredth anniversary of the establishment of the People's Republic of China in 1949.

The long-term and highly authoritative character of the IDDS helps explain the relationship between IDDS and "Made in China 2025." News reports in the U.S. sometimes give the impression that all of Chinese industrial policy is part of "Made in China 2025." This is not precisely true, but really, no harm is done.[6] Made in China 2025 did indeed signal the roll-out of a far more intrusive, comprehensive, and well-funded approach to industrial policy in

5 Moreover, provinces have the same administrative rank as ministries. The relationship between provinces and ministries is more collaborative, and less competitive, than that between ministries, but ministries still cannot issue commands to provinces.

6 Indeed, one of the defenses of China's industrial policy often made is the assertion that Made in China 2025 has been misunderstood, and that it is a relatively low-level document that is not authoritative enough to impose binding targets on any specific industry. This is a half-truth.

China. Moreover, Chinese government sources themselves sometimes fall into the habit of referring to the whole complex of policies as the "manufacturing super-power strategy."[7] By contrast, as explained earlier, the title of IDDS is somewhat misleading because of the way the word "innovation" is used. In fact, the IDDS, as a portmanteau policy, includes all the specific components of the sectoral industrial policies. Thus, the title "Made in China 2025," rather accurately reflects the goals of the entire range of Chinese industrial policies.

4.2.3. Cycles and Waves of Policymaking

The timeline of industrial policy shows the impact of the five-year planning process as well, albeit not in a mechanical way. Toward the end of each five-year period (that is, in 2005, 2010, 2015, and 2020), an effort to evaluate and re-think the existing policy approach gets under way. This process usually doesn't culminate in a new plan until the next year, the first year of the new Five Year Plan period. Thus, we saw the IDDS and a new SEI plan in 2016, the first year of the 13th Five Year Plan. Concurrent with the Five Year Plan, though, individual ministries and agencies are preparing their own plans, and these are usually finalized after the main FYP is issued. Sometimes, a sector or area needs additional strategic elaboration, and this may well occur in the following year. Thus, it is not surprising to see the Military-Civilian Fusion Plan and the Artificial Intelligence Plan emerging in 2017.

This policy cycle is constantly being adapted to new realities, though. Since the IDDS, in 2016, led to a strategic reorientation across-the-board, other sectors are being led to re-think their approach. From 2018, therefore, this has led to urgent 3-year action

7 In Chinese, *zhizao qiangguo zhanlue.* For example, the National Development and Reform Commission (NDRC 2018) issued a call to "fully bring into play the core and leadership role of state-owned enterprises in realizing the innovation-driven development strategy and manufacturing super-power strategy."

plans, essentially to bring the strategic guidance up to the end of the Five Year Plan in 2020. During 2020, as this is written, exercises are underway to evaluate the existing policy approach and suggest new guidelines for the 14th Five Year Plan (2021-2025). This plan will likely appear during 2021, and we do not have much indication, as of this writing, what changes will be made. However, under the dual impact of heightened strategic competition with the United States, and the disruption of the coronavirus pandemic, it is unlikely that any major shifts in direction will take place. When that plan is produced, it will serve as the foundation for scores of sectoral and regional Five Year Plans, which will be elaborated during 2021 and 2022.

4.3. Magnitude of the Policy

The preceding discussion implies that China is increasing its resources effort for industrial policy. This does indeed seem to be the case. It is extremely difficult to measure the total volume of resources going into Chinese industrial policy today. Resources flow through many channels, including direct investment by state-owned entities, tax breaks for R&D, as well as favored sectors and technology-intensive firms, regulatory preferences, and (usually short-term) protected markets. Policy instruments are discussed in the next chapter. Some are common instruments, used by many countries around the world. Others are unique, and exist only in the Chinese context. As it happens, one very large channel for industrial policy resources is a recent, distinctive invention of the Chinese government, the Government Industrial Guidance Funds.[8] The widespread introduction of this distinctive instrument coincides broadly with the roll out of the IDDS and can serve as an index of the increase in government effort associated with this third round of industrial policy.

8 Very little has yet been written about these funds (Huang 2019).

Figure 4.1: Government Industrial Guidance Funds: Cumulative Fund-Raising Scope

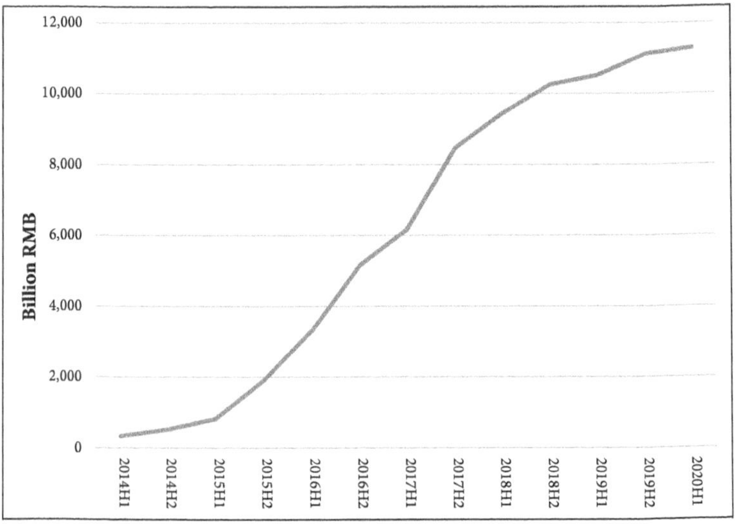

Sources: own elaboration compiled by the author from data supplied by Zero2IPO / Qingke Research Center (清科研究中心). Accessed at https://www.pedata.cn/. Some data may be behind paywalls.

As Figure 4.1 shows, Industrial Guidance Funds (IGF) took off after 2014. They grew rapidly through the end of 2018, and by June 30, 2020, the total designated fund-raising scope of all these funds was an astonishing 11,275 *billion* RMB —that is, 11.27 trillion RMB, or roughly USD $1.6 trillion. Figure 4.2 displays the time pattern of IGF development from a different perspective. A trickle of IGFs, starting in 2006, amounted cumulatively to only 317 billion RMB by the middle of 2014. Establishment of new funds then accelerated, and then took off in the second half of 2015, with over a trillion RMB in funds established in six-months, more than the cumulative total up until then. This extraordinary pace was sustained through the end of 2018, so that by that time a cumulative total of 10.2 trillion RMB (roughly USD $1.5 trillion) in IGFs had been established, representing over 11% of China's GDP. From the end of 2018, the pace of new fund establishment slowed substantially, even before the coronavirus in 2020. In three years, 2016 through 2018, China set aside well over a trillion dollars (8.3 trillion RMB) of fund-raising quota for IGFs.

Figure 4.2: New Government Guidance Funds: Designated Fund-Raising Scope

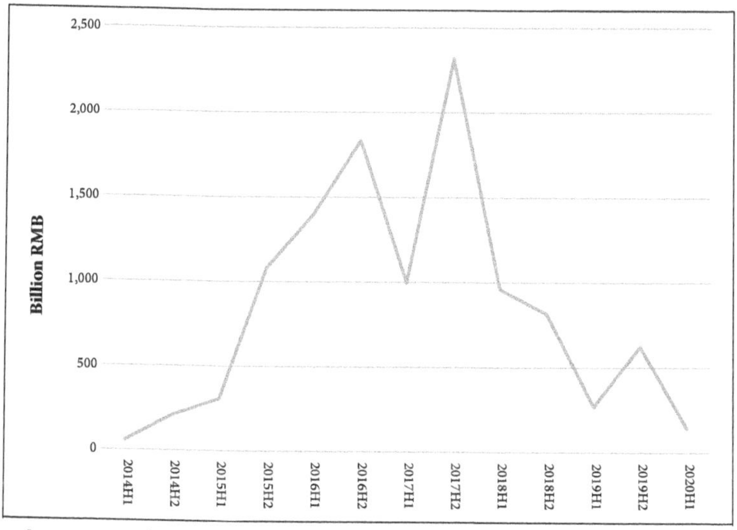

Sources: own elaboration compiled by the author from data supplied by Zero2IPO / Qingke Research Center (清科研究中心). Accessed at https://www.pedata.cn/. Some data may be behind paywalls.

To be sure, the numbers in the preceding figure represent the sum of the registered fund-raising plans of all of the IGFs. This is the first step in a process that includes actually raising the funds, and then making investments. Actual fund-raising lags behind plans, of course, and according to scattered 2019 press reports, amounts to about 60% of registered scope. Even so, that would be over 6% of GDP. There are substantial time-lags between when these programs are announced and when we expect them to have important economic effects.

The overall picture sketched by the numbers for IGFs is clear. Up until 2013 or 2014, China was making a substantial industrial policy effort, as indicated by the cumulative commitment to Megaprojects, SEIs, and other programs. Nonetheless, this effort was dwarfed by the resource commitment to the IDDS. Even if we confine our attention to the Industrial Guidance Funds, it is almost certain that the IDDS represents the greatest single commitment of government resources to an industrial policy objective in history. Moreover, many other instruments are in play, and it is likely that the resource effort suggested by their implementation has also increased since the inception of the IDDS. This IDDS seems to be a remarkable and unprecedented government effort.

4.4. Industrial Policy for a Technological Revolution: General Purpose Technologies

The inter-sectoral impacts of the IDDS are significant, but planners work with a fairly general conception of what those impacts will ultimately be, appropriately, since it is hard to predict specific applications. To understand how China's current industrial policy works, it is useful to look more concretely first at downstream sectors, where the new technologies will be applied, and then at upstream sectors that will produce high-technology inputs. A subsequent section looks at the relationship between China's industrial policy and the role of physical infrastructure investment.

4.4.1. Downstream: Three Areas of Application

The most attractive immediate applications of this new GP technology are in industry, transport, and military sectors. Industrial robots are already very important in the automobile and electronics industries, and they have the potential to spread much further. Indeed, the use of industrial robots and numerically controlled machine tools exemplifies a generation of industrial technology that has already been implemented in advanced economies, so-called "Industry 3.0." China is just a beginner in Industry 3.0, compared to countries like Germany, Japan and Korea which have already more-or-less universalized robots and digital control devices in automobile and electronics manufacturing. Now,

China seeks to leapfrog into Industry 4.0, and join the leaders. This means creating, implementing, and integrating clusters of industrial robots tied together with intelligent networks in order to automate entire manufacturing processes. This will be a big jump for China's manufacturing industry, which has been until recently heavily dependent on China's low-cost labor and often undertakes labor-intensive processes in preference to more expensive capital-intensive processes. This jump is the focus of the "Made in China 2025" component of the IDDS.

Transportation looks well-placed to be fundamentally transformed by the new GP technology package. Even before true autonomous vehicles (AV), transportation efficiency should be improved by various "Smart Cities" technologies: tuning traffic lights to respond to changes in traffic flows, for example. Moreover, fleets of trucks can be dispatched far more efficiently when each vehicle is tracked by sensors and integrated into a complete logistic effort. China is comparatively well advanced in these efforts. Hangzhou, the headquarters of Alibaba, is a candidate to be the smartest city in the world. Alibaba's "City Brain" program provides several layers of intelligent networking to facilitate transport and emergency services in the city. China's very high rate of infrastructure investment obviously provides China enormous opportunities to be an "early adopter" of transportation-related smart technologies (Naughton 2020).

Military applications for the technology triangle are also potentially enormous, and deeply destabilizing. Ever since the US victory in the first Iraq War ("Desert Storm"– February 1991), it had been clear that a "revolution in military affairs" was occurring. Desert Storm technologies were like Industry 3.0, based on individual smart weapons, which only the US at that time possessed. Today's AI-enabled technologies create a range of difficult-to-foresee situations in the Industry 4.0-type networked battlefield, including such things as massive intelligent swarms of drones. The completion of one of China's Megaprojects, the Beidou global positioning system, means China has now put in place one essential building block of contemporary military technologies. The 35th and final satellite of the system was placed in orbit in June 2020, providing complete global coverage. Military aspects of industrial policy are outside the scope of this essay, but it should be acknowledged that military and strategic concerns are key drivers of industrial policy decisions. In China, that means that the Military-Civilian Indus-try Fusion Program is an important constituent element of the IDDS.

4.4.2. Upstream: Key Sectors for the Technology Triangle

While the new GP technologies have broad effects downstream on every sector, it remains true that their mastery requires control of certain specific industrial sectors. It is no accident that Made in China 2025, with its emphasis on industrial robots, was the first salvo of the IDDS. More broadly, though, two sectors are essential for the new technological revolution: semiconductors (integrated circuits) and artificial intelligence. The two are very different.

Semiconductors are essential for each of the vertices of the triangle. Modern communications depend entirely on semiconductors, especially three key types: the processing chips in phones and other end-use terminals; the communications chips that link terminals and networks; and the server chips that power the nodes in the communications networks. Other smart networks are analogous to the phone network. Modern data storage is carried out entirely on semiconductors, in the ubiquitous memory chips that make everything else possible. Artificial intelligence obviously requires processors to work at all, and specialized processors to implement distributed AI, that is, efficient, low-electricity chips that provide just-enough "intelligence" required to make special-purpose local intelligent networks feasible. It is fair to say that the emergence of the AI-triangle is the result of the long-term increase in capability and decline in cost of ICs, following the fifty-plus years of Moore's Law.[9]

Semiconductor production capacity is not widely spread throughout the world. A small number of "fabs" produce the most advanced of the actual physical chips, notably Taiwan Semiconductor Manufacturing Corporation (TSMC), Samsung, and Intel. An equally small number of chip designers define the frontier of the most sophisticated chips, including Intel (again), Qualcomm, Samsung, and China's Huawei. Production of semiconductor manufacturing equipment is likewise concentrated in a handful of firms —American, Japanese and Dutch. However, there has been, until recently, a relatively open and free global market in most types of integrated circuits. Thus, most producers have had relatively equal access to the components needed for most types of electronic manufacturing. China has long been uncomfortable with its position in this industry. Large-scale semiconductor production was the last state-invested project standing when Zhu Rongji reduced industrial policy, and semiconductors were the first priority sector included in the revival of industrial policy. At the same time, the US (and, importantly, Taiwan) maintain export controls on semiconductor production technology to China, designed to keep China about two generations (i.e., 2-3 years) behind the technology frontier. To China's frustration, despite the expenditure of enormous sums of money, that gap has not been narrowed over the past thirty years.

The AI sector is very different. Knowledge production is concentrated: Google is the global leader by quite a bit. However, breakthroughs in A.I. programs are quickly published and available to a global audience. Advances in machine learning have steadily democratized the field of artificial intelligence. Almost anybody can participate, although developing deep expertise in specific applications is of course still extremely difficult and time consuming.

9 Moore's Law refers to the observation made by Gordon Moore in 1965 that the number of transistors packed into a given space would double every two years, doubling processing power, and/or reducing costs by half. Since 1965, this doubling has occurred regularly in less than two years, leading to the observation being dubbed a "law."

However, there are few barriers that prevent an ambitious newcomer like China from advancing rapidly in A.I. It depends entirely on the quality of human resources and the support they get.

4.4.3. Chinese Strategy: Upstream and Downstream Together

The Chinese strategy in the face of the new technological revolution is to invest in both upstream and downstream applications. Industrial policy-makers tend to take the "value chain" as a unit of analysis. (Chinese policy-makers absorbed the lessons of Global Production Networks into their own industrial policy framework.) For example the National Government IC Guidance Fund invests in the best indigenous firms at each stage of the semiconductor value chain (design, fab, packaging, equipment). Their objective from early on has been to grow domestic capability for each of the stages of the industrial value chain. A massive flow of resources into investment in the upstream stages of the value chain —for example in semiconductor design and production— is designed to increase capability and develop domestic supply.

At the same time, Chinese policy-makers are actively working to expand demand. Chinese government investment in infrastructure and information control provides it with an important early source of demand. It is no accident that Chinese firms like Hikvision have jumped to the lead in facial recognition technology: they have a patient and generous customer in the form of Chinese security services. We have already mentioned the business opportunities presented by Chinese government investment in "Smart Cities" infrastructure. Moreover, policy-makers believe the China has a unique ability to combine unified management of the Internet, ubiquitous sensors, telecommunications and smart transport/city networks, along with artificial intelligence. The US may be ahead in every one of these individual sectors, but the prospect for the US combining management and control of these networks is virtually zero. Therefore, China has the potential to reap the overall benefits of these general purpose technologies, catapulting it into a position parallel to, or ahead of, the United States. At the same time, the negative externalities of these technologies in enabling enhanced government surveillance and top-down control are welcomed by the Chinese government and have so far evoked little opposition among Chinese citizens.

The breadth of the strategy means that it is easily adapted to bring in additional elements. As described earlier, the SEI program has been modified to bring it more smoothly into the IDDS framework. The SEI program now focuses on five large industrial sectors, IT industry; industrial machinery; bio and pharmaceuticals; new energy vehicles and clean energy; and digital media. These are mostly downstream sectors where the projected economic opportunities and benefits of the new GP technologies are likely to be largest and quickest to materialize. With the obvious exception of semiconductors, the SEIs are generally not the core sectors technologically, but rather early adopters of new technologies. To be sure, their strengthened industrial capacities will also contribute to cost-effective implementation of new GP technologies more broadly. Military-civilian industry fusion is another case where cross-sector spillovers are a key justification for the policy: in this case, government as customer drives the growth of entire industrial sectors, with spill-on from civilian industry to the defense sector.

4.5. The Latest Component: New Infrastructure

The wave of new general purpose technologies interacts strongly with the provision of new types of infrastructure. Communications networks are an obvious example, and the current build-out of 5G telecom infrastructure is the focus of a great deal of attention worldwide. Transportation infrastructure needs to be built, and perhaps more importantly, upgraded to take advantage of new technologies. Energy infrastructure needs to be converted into "smart grids," in order to increase efficiency and reduce risks, and to drive transition to cleaner fuels. Infrastructure is extremely expensive, and the pace at which infrastructure should be built and upgraded will be a major determinant of economic gains going forward.[10] China has sustained a very high rate of infrastructure construction for over twenty years, and now the global economic crisis created by the coronavirus pandemic provides both new opportunities and new challenges.

The global economic recession in 2020 in the wake of the coronavirus economic crisis caused a shift in the cost-benefit calculus with respect to Chinese infrastructure policy. New types of infrastructure were already an integral part of the current wave of industrial policies. As countries around the world responded to the coronavirus crisis with various kinds of stimulus, it was not surprising that China also contemplated a stimulus program, but one built around the provision of "new infrastructure." While use of the term goes back at least to the end of 2018, a tentative round of new policies —potentially quite large— emerged during the first half of 2020, in response to the virus-induced recession. It is important to distinguish between strictly-defined "new-style infrastructure" and the broader definitions that could be employed to justify a large stimulus program. A narrower definition was laid out by Wu Hao of the National Development and Reform Commission (NDRC) on April 20, 2020 (Yang 2020). By this definition, new-style infrastructure would consist of:

1. The information infrastructure (or digital infrastructure). The communications network, including 5G telecom base stations, the internet of things, industrial internet and satellite communications; new technology infrastructure, including

10 In the past, China lacked infrastructure across-the-board, so a strategy of building infrastructure out ahead of demand was technically rather easy to execute, as long as the resources could be found. Now that an interregional grid of high-speed rail and expressways is nearing completion, and modern cities have largely been built, the question of where and how much infrastructure to be built is much more difficult to answer appropriately. More local knowledge and decision-making is likely indicated to make these decisions appropriately.

A.I., computing, and Blockchain; and computing infrastructure, including data centers and processing centers.
2. Integrated infrastructure. This means upgrading traditional infrastructure with the addition of internet, big data, and A.I. Examples include intelligent transport networks and intelligent energy infrastructure.
3. Innovation infrastructure. Science, technology, development, and research facilities.

While the first of these categories is relatively well-defined, many different kinds of activity can be included in the second category, upgrading traditional infrastructure. Moreover, these are the real big ticket items, on which hundreds of billions of dollars can be spent. While that may be acceptable if stimulus is urgently needed, it may be wasteful in the long-term if plans are not carefully laid out. In fact, policy-makers also floated a list of seven major sectors of "new infrastructure" that is more concrete than the NDRC definition (Wind Consulting 2020). These included:

1. 5G base stations and networks
2. Data centers
3. Artificial intelligence
4. Industrial internet of things
5. Electric vehicle charging stations
6. Ultra-high voltage (UHV) electric transmission lines
7. Intercity rail transit and urban subways

It can easily be seen that the first four of these are easily within the scope of the IDDS framework outlined in this chapter. The fifth, electric vehicle charging stations, is an effort to provide a piece of electric vehicle policy that has often been missing (repeatedly called for but rarely implemented). The last two areas of traditional infrastructure present opportunities for "smart" upgrading, although simple solutions are not necessarily readily available.

The possibilities of "new infrastructure" are impressive, but it is not a cure-all. In the first place, there is disagreement on the scope of stimulus needed: some policy-makers are wary of the expansion of debt that would be required for a major effort in this area. Infrastructure planning has long lead-times, even in China, and building infrastructure is a much less effective way to get money into the hands of households than other policies. Even those committed to a large program are looking for ways to get private sector buy-in that would lower the cost for the government. Second, there are technological issues still to be overcome. While the electricity company has already spent billions on UHV transmission, the technology has by no means been proven to be superior to existing technologies, nor does the use of UHV transmission automatically imply that grids are "smart." Indeed, they may be the opposite of "smart," since they have the potential to destabilize the overall grid. There is thus substantial debate and uncertainty surrounding the size and concrete implementation of the "new infrastructure." However, the decisions made with respect to "new infrastructure" are likely to be important influences on industrial policy over the next few years. As Chapter 1 stated, infrastructure construction multiplies the impact of industrial policy choices.

4.6. The Broad Development of Industrial Policy and Economic Strategy

Comparing these descriptions in this and the previous chapter, it is easy to see a pattern in the way in which Chinese central government industrial policy has evolved. In 2006, industrial policy began tentatively, at the "top" of the economy and at the bottom, or grass roots. At the top, the MLP suggested a broad range of possible directions in which the economy could be nudged; while at the bottom, the Megaprojects were a relatively small number of expensive projects funded by the government. In the years since 2006, industrial policy has expanded out both from the top and the bottom. Industrial policy has moved into the middle, and now permeates industrial investment and technology space.

From the top, policy increasingly is backed up with real resources —substantial and growing financial and other resource flows— so that policy becomes a way for the government to steer the real economy. Policy has evolved from something we can characterize as either "development strategy" or "indicative planning," into something that is clearly "industrial policy." Central policy is no longer merely a statement about possible evolutionary trends, primarily providing information to decentralized actors. It is today a statement of government intent to achieve certain outcomes based on the new technology opportunity set. Those outcomes can be defined very precisely (as in Made in China 2025), or they can be defined very loosely ("occupy the commanding heights of the new technological revolution"), but they are meant to be taken seriously.

From the bottom, government intervention has expanded from a few fully-funded projects, to sectoral interventions, and now to the point that government has sectoral policies for virtually every industrial sector. There are lists of target technologies to be mastered in emerging sectors; and the government expends and indirectly controls substantial resources for bottom-up restructuring of a vast range of sectors. The number of plans has multiplied perhaps a hundred-fold (and certainly many times tenfold), considering all the sectoral plans that are promulgated in the wake of the national five year plans. Thus, the space in the middle —between broad policy and selective investment— has increasingly been filled with a complex but comprehensive set of government steerage policies.

At the same time, industrial policy has become more broadly conceptualized as the application of advanced technology to many industrial sectors. That is, policies like Made in China 2025 and Internet Plus clearly envisage the application of new technologies to a broad range of sectors, including traditional industrial sectors. The same is true for the Artificial Intelligence Action Plan adopted in 2017. This gives a greater sophistication to industrial policy that in and of itself would be welcome. Policies have spread across a broader spectrum of the economy, meaning they have the potential to be less selectively targeted, and more "horizontal," encouraging the diffusion of new technologies without prejudging specific applications. This evolution was driven in part by recognized shortcomings within the earlier waves of industrial policy, and particularly of the SEI plan as originally promulgated. In reviews of the policy conducted around 2014-2015, it was recognized that many unrealistic targets had been promulgated, and a great deal of money had been wasted, and that a somewhat more "horizontal" approach to innovation would be more efficient. It was conceivable that recognition of these problems might have driven industrial policy toward a less targeted approach, or a "lighter touch" industrial policy.

Instead, the excitement generated by the increasing recognition of the potential revolutionary impact of the cluster of new general purpose technologies drove policy towards a more activist and increasingly interventionist stance. This was essentially a historic coincidence that fed the growing perception that rather than individual sectoral opportunities (as in the SEIs), China in fact faced a more general opportunity presented by the new technological revolution. Thus, the recognition of the broad applicability of these GP technologies was accompanied by an increased sense of urgency, and even greater priority given to fostering these technologies. As a result, recognition of the broad applicability of new technologies has not been followed by a "lighter touch" approach to specific sectors, quite the contrary. It has led to the cumulative targeting of broad technological changes *and* specific sectors. For example, industrial robotics has been targeted even as upgrading of traditional industrial sectors has been emphasized.

The result has been a greater sophistication of industrial policy, combined with a much broader scope of industrial policies. Industrial policy now permeates the Chinese economic landscape. The conception of technological and economic upgrading is more sophisticated and potentially more cost-effective than ever before. However, this sophistication is to a certain extent offset by the fact that government interventions have become more intrusive and more pervasive. The increased amplitude of these interventions is likely to be more distortionary. Moreover, due to the sheer multiplicity of intervention, it is extremely difficult to discern the size or net impact of these interventions. The indirect costs, doubtless substantial, are diffused through the economy and hard to perceive.

A parallel process of broadening the scope of industrial policy is discernable with regard to the attitude of policy-makers toward private businesses. Today, policy-makers have no problems supporting private businesses as part of industrial policies. This pragmatism is driven in part by a basic reality: much of the expertise in artificial intelligence and operating smart networks lies in the private sector. Salaries and profits are high, and the likelihood that the government can attract the talent it needs away from companies like Alibaba and Tencent is very low. It is far better, from the government's standpoint, to enlist these private firms in the national effort. It is now clear to everybody that Alibaba, Baidu, Tencent, and Huawei are all parts of the "national team," and that they must comply with "government guidance" to continue to be successful. Realistically, private firms have little choice, and substantial opportunity to benefit if they go along. The government is quite happy to spend money to further its objectives, and does not object if some of the money increases the profits of high tech companies. Alibaba's founder and CEO Jack Ma has even said that if the nation wants his company, they can have his company, implying that he will follow guidance in just about every aspect.

Even in defense industries, new policies are designed to open up as much as possible to private companies. The guiding philosophy of Military-Civilian fusion is to encourage civilian and private firm participation in military contracting. The objective is to tap into civilian high-tech expertise to strengthen the defense sector, and this necessitates greater openness to private business. To be sure, the bulk of resources in the defense industrial sector are still controlled by state-owned enterprises (SOEs). This highlights an important fact: while policy is probably closer to neutral toward private firms than it has been, the overall impact of industrial policies still favors SOEs. This is because SOEs are more easily assigned "missions" and given resources in pursuit of national goals. There has been a great deal of rhetoric about the importance of SOEs and their role as part of the "national team" supporting the IDDS lately. This reflects reality. However, support has gone to private companies as well, and overall this is a potential strength of the IDDS (State Council Office 2017).[11]

4.7. Key Success Factors

Whether the Chinese approach makes sense will be determined by the strength of two offsetting factors. On the positive side, AI and related technologies are becoming "general purpose" technologies that will revolutionize all production. Technological convergence —the increasing overlap of the component technologies that offer productivity-improving solutions to a wide range of sectors— is an external, largely exogenous, factor that increases the potential pay-off from industrial policy. A general purpose technology, such as electricity, is an advance that comes to be incorporated throughout the economy, driving up productivity growth for a generation or more. The occurrence of such an exogenous technological event strongly supports the fundamental rationale for industrial policy, which is that certain investments will generate spillovers (based on knowledge diffusion or other factors) that would not be captured by any private investor, and should thus be subsidized by government. As Pack and Saggi emphasize, "The ideal but rarely attained goal of industrial policy is the development of a general-purpose technology... [but] the discovery of such "general purpose technologies" is a rare event" (Pack and Kamal 2006:11). That means that the spill-over benefits (positive externalities) from these technologies are unusually large, potentially justifying government intervention to accelerate adoption.

11 This document specifically encourages private participation in railroad equipment, Internet Plus, Big data and robotics, on the ground that these sectors involve long and complex production chains. It also welcomes private participation in "Made in China 2025" demonstration zones and projects.

Whenever the technological externalities are larger and more significant, the case for government intervention is stronger. Market forces cannot be relied upon to produce optimal outcomes if the market cannot capture external economies. To the extent that a few key technologies might have economic benefits across a broad swathe of economic sectors, it may be reasonable for the government to promote those technologies. Certainly, this is what Chinese policy-makers are implicitly arguing. Moreover, because convergence in technologies is taking place, nobody is able to predict future technological configurations very well. The Chinese know they do not know what they are doing, but they are attempting to position themselves so that, when the revolution comes, they will have the skills to be a half step ahead, or at least not behind. Their gamble is that when new systems shake out, they will be well positioned to quickly adopt the most effective solutions, reap the productivity benefits, and develop newly competitive products and a more prosperous economy.

On the negative side, targeting industries at the technological frontier greatly increases risk and cost. There are no front-runners to emulate, and there is enormous uncertainty about which specific technological solutions will emerge as cost-effective and therefore dominant. There is significant risk of prematurely committing to a set of apparently superior technologies that are suddenly rendered obsolete by rapid technological change. It is worth stressing that China is not the science and technology leader in any of the component industries of the new technological revolution (with a few small, but important, exceptions such as quantum communications). It is hard to see that government targeting has any obvious advantages in a discrete case of industrial innovation. Indeed, it has generally been assumed that one of the reasons both Japan and Korea moved away from industrial policy when they did was that the importance and effectiveness of government targeting declined as their economies drew closer to the technological frontier. The task of developing specific technological solutions at the frontier was best diversified and left to individual companies. China's recent policy choices run in exactly the opposite direction, and completely counter to expectations based on the experience of forerunner economies (and industrial policy practitioners). The justification for this must lie almost entirely in whether or not there are complementarities among these emerging technologies which justify subsidizing early adopters.

It is conceivable that Chinese confidence in a new wave of transformative general purpose technologies will turn out to be wishful thinking. Past experience indicates that new GP technologies take decades to spread through the economy, and their impact often comes in ways that were poorly anticipated at the beginning. Whatever the future turns out to bring, China's current policy orientation will be extremely difficult to change, because it is backed by a strong enforced consensus. Overall, the IDDS is long-term and baked into a vast panoply of plans. It has been elaborated in many arenas, intertwined with various economic, military, and other objectives. The different approaches are like different "brands," that appeal to different constituencies, but are all part of a broad industrial policy initiative. To some constituencies, Military-Civilian Fusion is the most important component, a key to defensive strength. To other constituencies, research and the expansion of education are the most important components. Given the high degree of policy priority, and the strong interrelatedness between many aspects of these industrial policies, the whole complex is virtually impossible to change. Policy in China has a tendency to overshoot, generating destructive "great leaps." We cannot exclude that this will be the case with the IDDS as well. It is an enormous gamble, and the risk of overshooting is significant.

At the same time, as argued in Chapter 1, China is generally well positioned to be a global technological power. Many individual industrial policies may fail, and China may yet end up as a successful economy and a modern, influential global power. What is certain today, however, is that the process of China's emergence will be determined primarily by the interaction between an aggressive and interventionist government, on the one hand, and a robust business sector on the other, rather than through primarily market forces on their own. The gamble that China is taking today can best be understood in terms of the technological revolution. However, the probabilities of winning that gamble are likely more dependent on the specific instruments and policy tools that China adopts. That is the subject of the following chapter.

4.8. Conclusions

The adoption of the IDDS completed the dramatic transformation of Chinese industrial policy that began in 2006. China had already shown its willingness to adopt interventionist policies, and then to fund them generously. Now, China had found a broad and transformative rationale that further elevated the national significance of industrial policy. In this new conception, China's industrial policy had become part of a response to a technological revolution. Industrial policy was justified by the enormous potential externalities of a new general purpose technology. In a broader sense, it was also a way to combine China's vast human resources with traditional Chinese diligence and respect for education. As China's comparative advantage in (unskilled) labor-intensive manufacturing was fading, China hoped to move toward a new comparative advantage in high-skill and technology-intensive sectors. These broad and powerful rationales consolidated the support that top policy-makers were already giving to industrial policy, and put China firmly on a new path. Indeed, the attractiveness of this vision was such that it began to shape the type of institutions that China wanted to create. As the next chapter shows, the shaped of "economic reform" and institutional change has increasingly been shaped by China's industrial policy ambitions.

5

Instruments and Institutions

Previous chapters have shown that China's industrial policy initiatives expanded rapidly after 2006 and took on an increasingly sophisticated technological rationale after 2015. Following the refocus of industrial policy on a cluster of "general purpose" technologies, the economic rationale also became more coherent, in that instead of targeting a handful of promising dynamic sectors, the policies sought instead to foster the adoption of new general purpose technologies throughout the economy. This chapter builds on that foundation to show that China has also made an effort to use market-conforming instruments to achieve its industrial policy objectives. Indeed, Chinese policy-makers argue that they are creating a "market-driven, government steered" economy, essentially, a new model of an economic system. While the realization of this model is in practice likely to fall quite a bit short of the ideal, it is important to recognize the scale of the effort and the significance of the objective.

5.1 Combining Market Forces and Government Direction

Chinese policy-makers have rolled out a large number of new instruments, particularly financial instruments, to foster industrial policy. An important key to understanding these instruments is to recognize that Chinese policy-makers genuinely believe that these instruments combine market forces with government steerage, and that they will therefore be able to sidestep some of the disadvantages and costs of past command economy approaches to government steerage. Understanding this aspiration helps us to navigate the complex institutional landscape created by the recent introduction of many new instruments.

Chinese policy-makers genuinely believe that they are creating a system that merges the efficiency of the market with the ability of government to steer the economy. The "Made in China 2025" program explicitly states that one of the fundamental principles of the effort is that it is "market-driven, and government guided" (*shichang zhudao, zhengfu yindao*) (State Council 2015/a). The term *yindao*, generally translated as "guided" or "led," has a long history in Chinese Communist usage, usually referring to the "guidance" of public opinion. It implies something much stronger than simply influencing, rather a kind of sustained leadership, but preferably exerted subtly or indirectly. Thus, perhaps "steerage" gives a better sense of the meaning. While market forces are primary, and drive the economy, government steerage is seen as capable of turning market forces in one direction or the other. Similarly, the Ministry of Finance has described the integrated circuit government industrial guidance fund as "an organic combination of national strategy and the market mechanism" (Ministry of Finance 2018). Most recently, an important May 2020 programmatic document calling for further marketization also advocates concrete progress toward firmer steerage, to "move industrial policy toward generalized systems of preferences and functional approaches; strengthen support for technological innovation and structural upgrading; and strengthen the coordination between industrial policy and competition policy" (CCP Party Center and State Council 2020).[1] The reference is brief and abstract, but it indicates a desire to make industrial policy less inefficient and more market-conforming. At the same time, it makes clear that the overall commitment to industrial policy shows no signs of weakening.

The desire to combine government direction with the market economy has deep roots in China. A related concept may be found in (former World Bank Chief Economist and current Peking University professor) Justin Lin's "effective government and efficient market." It is expressed in the view that China's economic reforms have now been sufficiently successful in creating a market economy that they provide the basis for technology leadership under government guidance. The current Minister of Finance, Liu Kun, made his reputation by pioneering funds of this type in Guangdong province, and then championed them after he moved to Beijing (as Vice-Minister, and then Minister of Finance) in 2013. Thus, specific instruments for carrying out industrial policy are part of a broader effort to increase the amount of government steerage of a market economy. Whether or not it is in practice possible to impose so much government control on the economy *without* damaging market institutions remains to be seen, but Chinese policy-makers certainly *believe* that they are pioneering a new system of a government-guided market economy. Indeed, this seems to have become the most recent definition of the long-standing model of "a socialist market economy with Chinese characteristics."

At a minimum, we can say that if the expanded industrial policies described in the previous chapter had been implemented with the instruments typical of government administrative control in the past, it would already have created huge distortions with obvious negative economic effects. As it is, the current approach has at least allowed policy-makers to push resources into priority sectors while deferring some of the negative economic effects.

1 The original phrase is "推动产业政策向普惠化和功能性转型，强化对技术创新和结构升级的支持，加强产业政策和竞争政策协同."

More broadly, understanding the "market-driven, government-guided" system helps explain two fundamental features of the current Chinese approach: scattershot pragmatism and willingness to spend money.

5.1.1. Flexible, Pragmatic, and Opportunistic

China's "market-driven" approach supports a pragmatic commitment to multiple avenues and approaches. Really, almost nothing is ruled out from the outset. Thus, there is no ideological restriction on what can be done, and there is significant room for multiple, competing strategies and actors. The strategic approach is opportunistic. For example, for a brief period (roughly, 2013-2016), China through various agencies made a major effort to acquire foreign companies with significant technological expertise. After 2016, this offensive ran into problems both domestically (China experienced capital outflows that were too large for comfort) and internationally (as countries like the US and Germany rallied to protect their prime technological assets). As the window of opportunity for this campaign of acquisitions closed, a new emphasis on attracting and poaching international talent was adopted, to a certain extent as a substitute for corporate acquisitions. This can include simply paying sky-high salaries and allowing skilled engineers and designers to work from their home countries. For example, Yangtze Memory Technologies (YMTC), a generously funded start-up in Wuhan, China, that designs and manufactures 3-D NAND flash memory —relies on a global force of engineers in such places as Seoul.[2] This approach can also include innovative internationalized companies, such as the electric vehicle company Byton. Byton was "created" by a German veteran of BMW, and touts itself as a global company with many centers, but with production taking place in Nanjing in a partnership with state-owned First Automobile Works. It produced some impres-

2 See the company's website, ymtc.com.

sive concept cars in 2018, but is currently (early 2020) undergoing "reorganization" (Reuters 2018; Shirouzu 2018).[3]

As noted in the previous chapter, policy-makers have no problems supporting private businesses. At the same time, there has been a great deal of rhetoric about the importance of SOEs and their role as part of the "national team" supporting the IDDS. In June 2020, the body overseeing state firms re-emphasized their responsibility to be leaders in the technological upgrading process (Tang 2020). Thus, the reality is that increased support is going both to state firms and to private companies as well. A company like Alibaba is increasingly deeply entangled with the central government in a web of relationships, as customer, provider of funds, and co-investor. Even in the unlikely case that Alibaba preferred not to cooperate closely with the Chinese government, it would have few options to set an independent course. This flexibility is a potential strength, since the Chinese private sector is big, entrepreneurial, and possesses substantial technological resources. Policy-makers are happy to pick winners after the event, backing already successful firms in the expectation of raising them to be national champions.

Local governments have long played a prominent role in China's approach to development. In particular, local governments strategize different approaches to industrialization, and that has sometimes been beneficial to the development of high-tech industry. Today, the IDDS specifically says governments at all levels should play a part. What should be emphasized is that the difference in resources and incentives at the local and central government levels inevitably produce different strategic approaches, in ways that can be a strength for the overall policy. Moreover, with increasing use of a diverse array of financial instruments, central and local governments increasingly co-invest, sharing burdens and benefits of new investments. China is utilizing a somewhat market-friendly approach, along with a flexible attitude and strong commitment, to bring a wide variety of actors into the industrial policy realm.

3 See the company website at www.byton.com.

5.1.2. Spending and Raising Money

Chinese policy-makers are willing to spend a lot of money. China is the world's second largest economy, and government controls a large share of the economy, so the aggregate volume of resources available to be mobilized is extremely large. Moreover, technological mastery is seen as immensely valuable, both on strategic and economic grounds. This means that China is willing to pay a high cost to support development of advanced technologies. In a sense, Chinese policy-makers are willing to pay the "full sticker price." This attitude puts limits on the degree to which industrial policies can impose costly distortions on the economy. The biggest economic costs from aggressive government policy-making come when governments with weak revenue bases pursue objectives they can't, or don't want to, pay for. In those circumstances, hidden costs due to regulation or disguised protectionism build up, and rent-seeking behavior increases in their wake. By contrast, if the government pays for something that turns out to have no value, but it is fully funded out of taxes or central government borrowing, the cost is limited to the money wasted. There will be limited systemic damage or distortion, and this in turn limits the economic damage from very aggressive policies.

At the same time, government policy-makers certainly understand that they are paying a huge price for their industrial policies. They avoid publicizing these numbers, but since they are paying the sticker price (as it were), they are aware of the enormous costs involved. As a result, the Chinese government explores multiple avenues to leverage the funding they put into industrial policy. There are pursuing options of subsidy, capital injection, and guaranteed returns. In each of the instruments discussed later, there are multiple channels for the government to leverage its money. While this sometimes creates long-term risks, it is also smart policy-making in the short term. Strategic emerging industries are likely to be important investments and sectors in the future, so they will naturally attract investment. Government does not want to displace the investment that would come from private sources, it wants to encourage a larger and faster movement of resources into the sector (this is, of course, practically a definition of industrial policy). To make this happen, the government invests but also enacts preferential policies to attract additional investment and leverage its own commitment when possible. The Chinese government invests a lot directly *and* it leverages SOE and private investment in multiple ways *and* it provides preferential policies of various kinds. This marks a key point of separation between China's industrial policy and that of earlier examples such as Japan and Korea. Japan and Korea basically just provided preferential policies, then relied on large corporations to adapt their investment decisions to the information and incentives provides by preferential policies. In a sense, Chinese policy towards expenditure is a continuation and amplification of the flexible and opportunistic approach described in the previous section. The multiplicity of channels also makes it extremely difficult to track the funds flowing into targeted sectors.

5.2. Institutional Creation: Industrial Guidance Funds

Chinese policy-makers have actively set up new institutions in order to capitalize on the hoped-for possibility of combining market operations and government steerage. The most important new instrument is the "industrial guidance fund," which was introduced in the previous chapter. These basically seek to replicate U.S. experience with venture capital funds and other types of investment entities. These funds are set up to be "specialized," which means that they are to be run by professionals specialized in investment management.[4] Moreover, these professional managers are given clear incentive contracts, with relatively high-powered rewards for good performance. The funds are generally either limited partnerships —with a state-owned enterprise or government agency as the primary sponsor and managing partner— or a non-listed

4 Xiao Yaqing (head of SASAC), quoted in Xinhua News Agency (Xiao 2017).

joint stock corporation. One capsule description of the industrial guidance funds is as follows: "The government sets up a platform; central SOEs serve as sponsors; the [state] banks come in close behind; and social capital will follow."[5] These new institutions have their own shortcomings and risks, but they mark an improvement over past Chinese practice.

5.2.1. Industrial Guidance Funds – A Quantitative Sketch

Industrial guidance funds (IGFs) are new, but are already enormous. As shown in the previous chapter, IGFs grew rapidly through the end of 2018, and by June 30, 2020, had reached a total designated funding scope of 11.27 trillion RMB, or roughly USD $1.6 trillion. The total value of "guidance funds" was only a couple of hundred billion RMB at the end of 2014, concentrated in a handful of pioneering funds, such as the National IC Development Fund (first round) set up in that year.[6] The value is a stock, rather than a flow: it is the total fund-raising scope designated in the articles of agreement creating the fund. The figure is significantly larger than the flow of investment into projects during the course of the year. In the first place, not all the funds have raised all the money specified in the agreements. Furthermore, after money is raised, it takes time to appraise investments and begin to spend the money. In this sense, the figures may overstate the size of the financial resources mobilized. On the other hand, the database includes a substantial number of funds, about 20%, that do not have a fund-raising amount specified. These funds are obviously not included in the totals below. Even if their average size was only half of the funds with specified fund-raising, including the omitted fund, it would add another trillion RMB to the scale of resources.

5 "*Zhengfu datai, yangqi faqi, yinhang genjin, shehui ziben suiting*" (Chen 2015).

6 These data are calculated by the author from the commercial database maintained by Zero2IPO (清科研究中心). Accessed at https://www.pedata.cn/. Some data may be behind paywalls.

As Table 5.1 shows, the majority of IGFs are controlled at local levels. As of mid-2020, the central government has not quite 2 trillion in funds; provincial governments control 3.3 trillion, and municipal governments have 3.7 trillion RMB. Municipal governments typically oversee the bulk of industrial activity in China, so this distribution is not entirely surprising. Local funds are considerably smaller than central government funds, of course. Guangdong pioneered the development of these funds. The first local government funds date back to 2000, whereas the first central government fund was only established in 2013. However, the establishment of the central IC fund in 2014 marked the beginning of a new era, and funds at all levels proliferated strongly from 2015.

Table 5.1: Total Value of Industrial Guidance Funds (2020)

	Trillion RMB	Percent
National/Central	1.96	19%
Provincial	3.30	32%
Municipal	3.72	36%
County	1.34	13%
Total	10.32	100%

Sources: own elaboration compiled by the author from data supplied by Zero2IPO / Qingke Research Center (清科研究中心). Accessed at https://www.pedata.cn/. Some data may be behind paywalls.

When the funds are established their investment orientation is described. Descriptions are inconsistent and sometimes overly broad. However, in a random sample of 10% of all funds in mid-2018, in reading the description and assigning the investment strategy to a category, the groups shown in Figure 5.1 clearly emerge. About 38% of funds by number are designated for broad, multi-sector "high tech" investments, such as SEIs, "new growth drivers," or related. Another 12% are single-sector funds for a sector such as advanced materials or integrated circuits that is clearly high-tech. A third large category includes advanced manufacturing and industrial upgrading, which accounts for 11% of funding. Consolidating these three categories gives us a total of 61% of funds are for high technology industries, broadly considered. Promotion of specific service sectors, including tourism and culture, accounts for another 13% of funds (although these are typically much smaller than the industrial funds). Another 14% of funds are for infrastructure, energy and environmental alleviation. Finally, about 4% of funds are devoted to small and medium enterprise development, which depending on the fund managers could be oriented toward high-tech start-ups or toward ordinary small-scale firms. A large number of funds either do not disclose their sectoral orientation, or are so broad as to be meaningless. Overall, at least 61%, and more likely about two-thirds, of IGFs are for purposes directly related to industrial policy priorities.

5.1 Sectorial Orientation of Industrial Guidance Funds

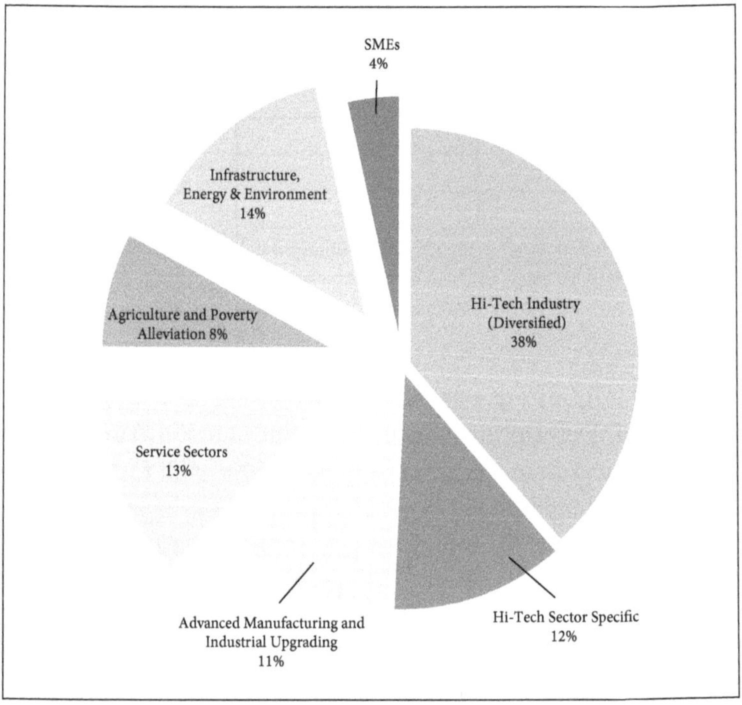

Sources: own elaboration compiled by the author from data supplied by Zero2IPO / Qingke Research Center (清科研究中心). Accessed at https://www.pedata.cn/. Some data may be behind paywalls.

The largest IGFs are shown in Table 5.2 below. There are several huge central-government-run funds. The two rounds of funding in the IC Industry Development Fund together add up to 338.7 billion RMB (about USD $50 billion). The first round, of 138.7 billion, was fully invested by the end of 2018, and a second round was launched, raising an additional 200 billion. The other large central government funds mainly target central state-owned enterprises. They reflect a policy of using financial resources to restructure state firms, moving away from traditional administrative control, and towards a state-owned holding company approach (See Section 5.3.2). Large local government funds are somewhat harder to track. A number of provinces, including Shandong and Sichuan, have announced very large funds, but the announcements later proved to be aspirational targets for all of the different funds in the province. Shenzhen runs one of the largest funds (Kunpeng Fund), and Guangdong is home to a large collection of funds such that in the aggregate it probably controls a larger volume of financial resources than any other province.

Table 5.2: Largest Industrial Guidance Funds (2020)

Fund Name	Level	Scale (Billion RMB)
Integrated Circuit Fund (both rounds)	National	338.70
Optical Valley Fund (Wuhan)	Municipal	250.00
Government-Enterprise Cooperation Fund	National	180.00
Central SOE Innovation Fund	National	150.00
Kunpeng Fund (Shenzhen)	Municipal	150.00
National SOE Adjusment Fund	National	130.00
Shanxi Taihang Fund	Provincial	105.00
Jiangxi Development and Upgrading Fund	Provincial	100.01
Beijing Investment Guidance Fund	Provincial	100.01

Sources: own elaboration compiled by the author from data supplied by Zero2IPO / Qingke Research Center (清科研究中心). Accessed at https://www.pedata.cn/. Some data may be behind paywalls.

5.2.2. Key Institutional Features of IGFs

Industrial guidance funds have a common structure.[7] They are incorporated as separate entities, typically as limited partnerships or joint stock corporations (unlisted), although other contractual forms are also permitted. The benefit of IGFs in the eyes of government policy-makers —and to a certain extent in reality— is that they create clearly specified responsibilities and incentives, and therefore permit professionalization and market-responsive behavior. There are six key institutional features of IGFs. These are (a) initiating party and managing agency; (b) share-holders and limited partners; (c) designated sectoral strategy; (d) designated investment strategy; (e) explicit incentive system; and (f) subsidization channels. In this section, we will describe each of these features, in general, and then illustrate with the example of the National Integrated Circuit Fund (first round), and sometimes other funds. The National IC Investment Fund was one of the first and biggest industrial guidance funds, set up in September 2014. Since the IC Fund was set up early and invested quickly, it has completed fund-raising and expenditure of the first round, and the second round was launched in 2018. Thus, we have a relatively good understanding of its operations, and we will use it as an example of the basic features of IGFs.[8]

(a) Initiating Party and Managing Agency

Each IGF has an initiating party, or sometimes two. The initiating party is a government agency which takes responsibility for creating the fund and then designates an agency as the managing agency. Typically, but not always, this managing agency is a

7 Many of these common features are mandated in the rules and regulations laid out by National Development and Reform Commission (NDRC 2016).

8 Because the IC Fund was a pioneer, some of its features may turn out to be modified in subsequent funds.

department or subsidiary of one of the initiating parties. The managing agency is thus similar to the General Partner in a Venture Capital firm. The IGF will also have Limited Partners (discussed below) that provide capital but are not directly responsible for operations, or for losses beyond their own capital contribution. The managing agency is responsible for day-to-day operation of the fund. It will typically have an Investment Committee that decide on individual investments. Depending on the size of the investment, the Investment Committee will be internal to the managing agency, or for large investments, and will operate at the fund level and include the limited partners. The regulations for IGFs specify that the government body responsible for establishing the IGF is not allowed to interfere in the day-to-day operations of the fund: that is the responsibility of the managing agency alone.

For example, the national IC Fund was established by Ministry of Industry and Information Technology (MIIT) and the Ministry of Finance as joint initiating sponsors. The Ministry of Finance contributed 36 billion RMB, and 8 enterprises joined on creation as initiating shareholders, that is, as sponsors. The initiating sponsors called on the investment bank subsidiary of China Development Bank, CDB Capital, to put together a managing agency for the fund. This new agency, called Huaxin Investment Management Company, is headed by a former vice president of China Development Bank. According to industry sources, the decision to appoint a head with a background in finance, rather than in electronics, was made in order to signal that the fund was serious about earning a return on its investment. The managing agency is itself a corporation, with a total equity capital of 120 million RMB. Most of the funds came from the national initiating sponsors, but the Shanghai Digital Industry Group, an instrument of the Shanghai Pudong government, also took a stake in Huaxin ("representing the Shanghai government"). The managing agency's capital, in this case, was equal to 0.1% of the initial expected fund-raising scope (later augmented) of 120 billion RMB (SDI Group 2018).

Another large fund example comes from the creation of the massive 300 billion RMB National Strategic Emerging Industries

(SEI) Fund on June 12, 2018. In this case, the National Development and Reform Commission (NDRC), the erstwhile planning agency, and the Bank of Construction were the joint initiating parties. This fund was set up eight years after the SEI program was officially announced, and after scores of local SEI funds have already been set up, so it should be viewed as part of a recommitment by the central government to the support of SEIs (Li 2018). This time sequence is quite different from that of the National IC Fund, which was the forerunner of a new wave of IC investment, and the creation of which was followed by the creation of many local IC funds.

Local funds are created through a similar process, with the city or provincial government playing a much stronger overall role.[9] For example, Wuhan is one of four areas designated by the national plan to develop the IC industry. The Wuhan (city) Economic Development Investment Corporation is the initiator of a 30 billion RMB fund, called the Hubei (province) IC Industry Fund. Fiscal agencies at the province (Hubei), city (Wuhan) and local development zone (Eastlake High technology New Zone) all contributed as initiating sponsors (Zhongguo Ribao 2015). The fund then brought in multiple investors and also signed a strategic cooperation agreement with CDB Capital to provide some financial management services. Nanjing city government has an even more ambitious program, involving the attraction of multiple foreign companies, including Cadence and Synopsis among EDA companies and a subsidiary fab of TSMC. In Nanjing, as in Wuhan, the IC Fund is just one strand in a multi-stranded municipal effort that includes new development zones, tax breaks and subsidized rents, and direct investments. Nanjing is much more focused on cooperation with existing domestic and multinational firms than Wuhan. The Nanjing city government established a 50 billion RMB IC Industry Development fund in December 2016, which combined with the 10 billion RMB funds established by its Jiangbei New District (which

9 Provincial governments also play a role, but municipal governments are typically much more hands on with this type of economic development policy.

has a strategic focus on ICs) gave it a total of 60 billion RMB available. In July 2018, a new IC fund of USD $20 billion was established by Nanjing.[10] The most sophisticated and activist local governments —including those in Wuhan, Nanjing and Shanghai— establish IGFs as integral components of local government development plans.

(b) Share-holders and Limited Partners

Upon establishment, IGFs raise funds by bringing in a group of limited partners (or alternatively as equity shareholders). Table 5.3 shows the funding structure for two of the largest and most important central government IGFs. For the National IC Fund, seven enterprises, all SOEs, bought into a secondary offering —functionally similar to coming in as limited partners— three months after the Fund was set up, creating 99 billion in shareholder equity. The Central SOE Structural Adjustment Fund was established in 2017, and the first round of fund-raising was closed when 131 billion RMB had been raised. In the case of the National IC Fund (first round), not only was the entire amount of capital quickly raised, it was augmented by additional issuance of preferred stock (described below). Moreover, in the case of the National IC Fund, the first round funds have been fully invested, and a second round of fund-raising was launched in 2018, and quickly closed after raising 200 billion.

10 "As an IC Chip city is being created, a 20 B. USD investment fund is being set up, comparable to the first phase of the Big Fund [in Chinese]" (International Electronics Commerce 2018).

Table 5.3: Funding of Large Central IGFs

Central SOE Structural Adjustment Fund (2017)		National IC Fund (First Round 2014)	
RMB Billions		RMB Billions	
Partner	Investment	Partner	Investment
Jianxin (Bank of Construction Investment)	50	Ministry of Finance	36
Chengtong Corp (primary sponsor)	30	CDB Capital	22
China Merchants Group (SOE)-Shenzhen	20	China Tobacco Monopoly (SOE)	11
Sinochem (SOE)	5	Beijing Yizhuang International (local SOE)	10
China Armaments Group (SOE)	5	Wuhan Financial Holding (local SOE)	5
Beijing Finance Street Investment (SOE)	5	Shanghai Guosheng Investment (local SOE)	5
Shenhua Coal Group (SOE)	5	China Mobile (SOE)	5
China Mobile (SOE)	5	Others	5
China Transport Construction (SOE)	5		
China Zhongche (SOE)	1		

Sources: own elaboration based on Lan (2018) and Gu (2017).

In both these big national funds, all of the limited partners were SOEs. The SOE Structural Adjustment Fund was initiated in September 2016 by the Chengtong Corporation, a central government SOE that has been converted into a state-run investment corporation. This may be a special case. The IGF is established specifically in order to re-organize central SOEs, so in this case the limited partner central SOEs are contributing to a fund that directly or indirectly works for their own ultimate benefit. Thus, strong participation by central SOEs in this case is not surprising. Nonetheless, we have to note the very large contributions by the Bank of Construction and the China Merchants Group (primarily a bank holding company). In addition, the China Postal Savings Bank played a large role in initial organization of the fund, though it was not ultimately one of first-round stakeholders. While these financial enterprises are technically central SOEs, they are unlikely to benefit directly from restructuring carried out by the fund, and they are participating as financial investors.

The National IC Fund also shows the dominance of SOEs among limited partners, although a number of patterns are apparent. Certain limited partners (the tobacco monopoly and perhaps China Mobile) seem to have been assigned the role of limited partners because they are cash-rich businesses. In addition, three local SOEs —one each from Beijing, Shanghai, and Wuhan— have become limited partners because they expect their locality to benefit from the fund's investments. This is especially obvious in the case of Wuhan, which has received massive investments from the National IC Fund in the years since its establishment. In addition, the National IC Fund, in the first quarter of 2015, issued an additional 40 billion in preferred stock, which was purchased primarily by the People's Insurance Company of China (PICC), creating a total fund value of 138.72 billion. Thus, in one sense we could say that the Ministry of Finance's injection of government funds was multiplied by 3.85. On the other hand, all of the money came from state-owned entities, so it was still all government money. Some of the local funds claim to have private participants, but the information on partner identities is scarce and the amounts appear to be small.

Clearly the dominance of SOEs as limited partners is not because policy-makers discourage private participation. Quite the contrary, private firms are explicitly encouraged to participate in industrial policy initiatives and the IGFs have repeatedly been praised as a vehicle that potentially can draw in private funds. The fact that there are so few cases of private firm participation shows that the incentive structures are not what they appear to be. The Chinese government recognizes that it needs to make it worth the while of private firms to participate, and they do not shrink from providing benefits directly to private firms, but they do not seem to have found a way to do so. A policy on encouraging private investment (not just in IGFs) was adopted by the State Council Office in September 2017, and it quickly gets to the point, after saying that private firms should be brought into industrial policy priority sectors: "We should bring into play the function of fiscal funds in spurring [private sector investment], using diverse methods such as investment subsidies, capital injection, or setting up investment funds, to attract a broad swathe of social capital, support enterprises in increasing the magnitude of their technological effort, in order to increase the input into keypoint projects in critical areas like integrated circuits or in [technological] weak links" (State Council Office 2017:79).[11] In other words, private firms are welcome to participate as investors in the funds and the funds are encouraged to invest in private firms in pursuit of their objectives.

(c) Designated Sectoral Strategy

Every fund has a "purpose." Upon establishment, it declares the investment strategy it will follow, and these strategies are a matter of public record. However, as the quantitative data presented above show, most funds intend to invest in a relatively broad range of high tech, strategic, or "new growth driver" sectors. In practice, IGFs may have quite a bit of flexibility. There are also a number of special purpose IGFs devoted to, for example, poverty alleviation. These can be large and important, but are a modest share of overall IGFs. Clearly, there is enormous diversity in the sectors targeted and invested in by IGFs.

Once again, the IC Industry Fund makes a good example because its strategy is relatively clear and its actual track record is already available. The National IC Fund was established relatively early, specifically because of the realization that IC fabs, in particular, were enormously capital-intensive and expensive. As one source put it, "with a big investment you can make a lot of money; a medium-sized investment can't turn a profit; and small investments just bleed red ink" (China Merchants Equity Analysis 2014).

11 This document specifically encourages private participation in railroad equipment, Internet Plus, Big data and robotics, on the ground that these sectors involve long and complex production chains. It also welcome private participation in "Made in China 2025" demonstration zones and projects.

The core purpose of the National IC Fund was therefore to help companies scale up. The fund was explicitly centralizing, because only the National Fund could possibly mobilize funds on this scale. The goal was to quickly take existing companies and projects and provide them with ample funding to complete large-scale projects quickly.

According to industry analysts, the initial intention of the IC Fund was to invest about half of its funds into new chip fabs, 20-30% into supporting consolidation through mergers and acquisitions, 10% into chip design, and smaller amounts into packaging and testing, equipment and materials, and IC applications (China Merchants Equity Analysis 2014). The goal was to invest at all stages of the production chain, but especially in those segments where large-scale capital infusions would do the most good, i.e., in chip manufacturing ("fabs"). The National IC Fund quickly followed through on this strategy. They invested in what became Tsinghua Unigroup's subsidiary Unigroup Spreadtrum and RDA. In this transaction, with the help of the National IC Fund's first investment, Tsinghua Unigroup acquired the two best private Chinese companies engaging in communications IC design, Spreadtrum and RDA, and merged them into a single company. Whether this was a smart move is a controversial question. The merger combined two very different companies with visionary entrepreneurs and very different corporate cultures into a single, less agile company. The founders of both companies eventually left the new combined entity. On the other side, Intel Corporation has invested in this company, perhaps partly to placate Chinese industrial policy-makers and also to foster the adoption of its mobile chips, which are otherwise not doing well in the international market (Cision 2018).

Next, the IC Fund invested in SMIC (Semiconductor Manufacturing International Corporation), the largest mainland-based pure play fab. IC Fund investment helped SMIC through an expansion phase. Subsequently, the IC Fund invested in Jiangsu Changjiang Electronics Company (JCET), China's largest indigenous packaging and testing company (third largest in the world).

Finally, the IC Fund invested in AMEC (*Zhongwei Bandaoti*), China's largest semiconductor equipment company. Thus, within the space of about twelve months, China's National IC Fund had invested in the largest company in each of the four major links in the integrated circuit production chain: design, manufacturing, package/test, and equipment. It infused money into each step along the chain.

Subsequently, the National IC Fund began to search out new projects, and also took stakes in a broad range of semiconductor-related firms. In the fourth quarter of 2017 and first half of 2018, the National Fund invested almost 25 billion RMB in 15 separate investments in the secondary market (Integrated Micro Web 2018). Whether this was a well-thought out program to strengthen specific firms, a quiet way to prop up the stock market during a time of difficulty, or just a way to spend down the remainder of the first phase funding is not entirely clear. Perhaps ironically, the spread of local IC Industry IGFs soon meant that investment once more became dispersed among a large number of firms, many of which duplicate each other's efforts and others that are unlikely to attain economic scale. China industry representatives purport to be unconcerned by this development. They argue that an intensely competitive environment has been created, at least among companies on the fringes of the industry. Most of them will go bankrupt, they acknowledge, but some will survive, and it will be relatively easy for the National Fund to come in and support the emerging survivors. In addition, their funding can help the new "national champions" buy up the failing companies.

(d) Designated Investment Strategy

IGFs must specify their investment strategy, i.e., select investment types. They can be established, at one extreme, as a Fund of Funds (many are), deferring the investment strategy decision to their subsidiary funds. At another extreme, they can be angel investors or venture capital funds, investing early in start-ups. In between, they can designate themselves as private equity funds, investment funds, mezzanine investors, or investors in secondary market.

The National IC Fund is a "growth fund." It does not invest in start-ups, either as an angel investor or a venture capital fund. Rather, it serves as a late-stage private equity firms, assisting existing firms to grow robustly and reach economic scale (China Merchants Equity Analysis 2014). This is entirely consistent with its sectoral focus and strategy. As described earlier, the IC Fund took 15 positions in the secondary market in just over nine months in late 2017 and the first half of 2018. Obviously, this means the national IC Fund is co-investing with many companies. This allows them to claim that they have "mobilized 514.5 billion in dispersed social capital." Under the circumstances, this claim is rather nonsensical, although conceivably other IGFs might plausibly make such a claim. However, the IGFs, by investing in listed firms, clearly signal that a stock is looked on favorably by at least some part of the government. Some opportunistic investors will certainly try to follow IGF investments —or front-run them— in order to benefit from the stock's appreciation. This increases finance available for these firms, while also creating new kinds of risks and costs.

(e) Explicit Incentive System

Ultimately, the behavior and performance of IGFs depend on the incentives that are given to investment managers. Unfortunately, the specific contractual documents that govern managerial incentives are not generally publicly available, so we don't have a precise understanding of these incentives. However, we do have a few pieces of relevant information that provide a rough understanding of what the incentives look like.

First, we have had many indications that IGFs target extremely low rates of return. A Shanghai fund manager has been quoted as saying that as long as the fund gets its money back, it does not matter if it makes a profit. The National IC Fund is known to have targeted a 5% rate of return. However, according to industry sources, the Fund had to acknowledge that it would not be able to make such a return, and it set up a separate "Strategic" sub-fund with a target rate of return of zero percent, along with the "Commercial" sub-fund with the 5% target rate of return.

Second, fund managers have told industry sources that there are high-powered incentives available for those who achieve more than the target rate of return. In other words, investment managers get to split returns above the targeted rate, according to some generous formula. It might be reasonable to conclude that fund managers get rewarded if they produce a substantial return, but probably are not punished if they fail to achieve a positive return.

A third source on incentives comes from the NDRC model regulations. The regulations specify the basis on which investment managers may be rewarded, without providing any quantitative details. The list of factors that should determine compensation to the investment manager are, in this order: (1) total value of assets under management; (2) past investment return; and (3) whether past investment activity is consistent with government industrial policy guidance (NDRC 2016). In other words, in the NDRC's framework, while managers can be rewarded for positive returns, growing total assets in conformity with industrial policy guidelines is at least as important. Industry sources suggest that for the IC Fund, import substitution, acquiring intellectual property, and building a domestic industry are the key objectives, and that managers understand this. These diverse objectives suggest that rate of return will not, in fact, be the predominant success indicators for managers of the IC Fund.

(f) Channels for Subsidization

To complete the institutional description, we need to take into account the ways in which government uses the IGF institutions to subsidize investment in targeted sectors. After all, the purpose of these funds is to promote investment, and not just through providing superior information or access to efficient capital markets: the purpose is to subsidize investment in the targeted sectors. A preliminary reconnaissance indicates the following channels are among the more important ways that IGFs seek to subsidize investment:

a) Government provides free, patient capital as the initial investor in the funds. While the funds are structured as investments that retain or increase their value, the reality is the government provides money under conditions that make it clear that it is in no hurry to get it back. Government waits patiently, its investment making an implicit zero return, thus essentially providing interest-free loans to the investment.
b) Government sponsorship is used to attract low-interest loans to complement direct investment financing. With the IGF providing equity capital, leverage can be attracted from state-owned banks. For example, China Development Bank has committed 1.4 trillion RMB to strategic emerging industries over 5 years, and this would mainly be provided as bank loans to support the activities of the SEI IGF. We do not know if specific undertakings have been made with respect to the interest rate, but presumably financing would be ample and interest rates set on the assumption that these are super-safe government-backed borrowers.
c) Government provide explicit and implicit guarantees for investments. One of the forms of explicit guarantee was brought to light when the People's Insurance Company of China (PICC) purchased 4.1 billion RMB worth of preferred stock in the National IC Fund. In discussing this investment, it was pointed out that in the State Council regulations establishing the National IC Fund, there were provisions for the Ministry of Finance to set aside an additional sum of money to pay the fixed return on the preferred stock if profitability fell below target. It is not clear if this fund can indemnify *any* investor participating in a failed IC fund investment, or if it is limited to preferred stock or

other particular situations (21st Century Economic Herald 2016).

Clearly, there are multiple channels of subsidization built into the IGF structure. In addition, one must assume that the government will be far more willing to write off certain kinds of failed investment than would private investors, and this also provides an important element of subsidy for risky investments.

5.3. The Funding Hierarchy

Although IGFs are the newest and largest industrial policy instrument on the scene, they are embedded in a hierarchy of government-run financial institutions.

5.3.1 State-owned Banks

As in any economy, the banking system plays a fundamental role. In China, while all the large, state-run commercial banks provide finance to government industrial policy objectives, the government-run development banks play a special role. China Development Bank, in particular, combines a mission to provide policy lending with significant financial expertise. As seen in the discussion of the IGFs, China Development Bank has been an important actor as initiator and, especially through its CDB Capital investment bank subsidiary, as managing agency, of many large IGFs (CDB 2019).

This by no means exhausts the role of state-owned banks. Indeed, the commitment from the banking system inevitably sets the overall framework for the volume of resources flowing through the overall industrial policy program. A glimpse of the overall funding structure was provided when the new Strategic Emerging Industries (SEI) Plan for the 13th Five Year Plan (2016-2020) was promulgated in 2016. An ambitious new industrial guidance fund, the National SEI Fund was announced, with a fund-raising scope of 300 billion RMB (Li 2018). However, the actual take-up was much more moderate, with first-round funding amounting to 30 billion RMB. Even more striking, though, was the magnitude of the five-year commitments made to the funds by China's main banks. These were reported to be:

China Development Bank—not less than 1.4 trillion RMB
China Export-Import Bank—not less than 800 billion RMB
China Construction Bank—not less than 300 billion RMB

Total of these three banks: not less than 2.5 trillion RMB over 5 years, or over USD $350 billion RMB (Li 2018). Over a period of five years, the state banks promised to provide more than eight times as much money as the fund's targeted fund-raising scope. This commitment may include either capital investment or lending from the banks. Note also that these are commitments specifically to the National SEI Fund, specified in memoranda of cooperation signed between the NDRC, as the initiator of the fund, and the government banks. In addition, of course, each of these banks invests in many other Industrial Guidance Funds (IGF), often local, through various channels. Thus, the state-owned banks should be expected to invest a much larger total sum in national SEIs than the amounts to the single national fund. Overall, a great deal of the money comes from the state-owned banking system, and it flows through many channels.

5.3.2. State Investment Corporations

China's state-owned enterprises (SOEs) have undergone many rounds of reorganization in the past forty years. Since the end of 2003, SASAC (The State Asset Supervision and Administration Commission), with its central and local government divisions, has been the "ownership agency" that exercises ultimate authority over SOEs. Central SASAC has re-organized its firms into about 100 industrial holding companies.[12] Since 2013 a new round of SOE re-organization and reform has stressed "managing capital rather than assets." This program envisages delegation of more authority to these holding companies, and the conversion of many of them into "investment-authorized entities." This means that they have more financial autonomy and are expected to make and professionally manage investments, especially investments in industrial policy-related projects and firms. In some cases, these new entities shed any direct industrial functions, and in some cases they are becoming new conglomerates with both industrial and financial functions and subsidiaries. This is part of a broader trend toward the financialization of government control of the state enterprise sector. The purest expression of this is when top-level SOEs are converted into "State Capital Investment and Operations Companies" (SCIOs). These are not themselves IGFs, but are quite often the creators and sponsors of IGFs.

Examples of this type of SCIO include Chengtong 诚通, the initiator of the huge SOE Structural Adjustment Fund, and Guoxin 国新, initiator of many IGFs, including China Venture Capital. These SCIOs, in other words, play a role rather similar to that of the investment bank subsidiaries of the big state-owned banks. They are active players, well-endowed with government money, and with strong mandates to carry out industrial policy objectives while also, hopefully, making money. They are important strategic players at the top of the funding hierarchy.

5.4. Institutions and Issues: Evaluation

The previous section showed the substantial attention paid by Chinese policy-makers to create an institutional framework for IGFs that would allow them to combine market operation and government guidance. There are significant elements of institutional

12 Central government ownership of banks and other financial institutions is exercised through an entirely separate system, with the Huijin Corporation serving as the bank holding company.

innovation in IGFs that make them worthy of note, and they represent a serious effort to replicate some of the best features of American capital markets. In particular, separate IGFs are being set up to target different points in the enterprise life cycle, including start-ups, early expansion, mezzanine funding, and growth phases, each of which has different risk characteristics and different funding needs. Managers of individual IGF funds are specialized, can accumulate experience in specific industries and strategies and, in theory, have high powered incentives that reward them for finding high pay-off investments. These funds are far more sophisticated than old-style Chinese government investments, to say nothing of traditional "central planning."

At the same time, there are numerous shortcomings to this institutional set-up. While the IGFs portage into China institutional features that have developed in the U.S.'s market economy, they transplant them into a very different institutional environment. In fact, the industrial policies they are part of actually worsen said institutional environment in many respects. Moreover, this institutional environment and the way government activism affects it are well known to economic actors in China (and for that matter, in the U.S.). Therefore, there are substantial reasons to believe the long-run effectiveness of the IGFs will fall far short of the hopes invested in them by policy-makers. There are four, closely related, problems that are most important: dominance of government funding; implicit government guarantees; soft corruption; and creation of investment bubbles. In addition, we can point to two other incentive problems.

5.4.1. Dominance of Government Expenditure

As described earlier, an important objective of the institutional design of IGFs was the desire to limit government expenditure, to allow "steerage" by concentrating government outlays on the margin, deflecting investment expenditure into priority sectors. The funding arrangements for the national IC fund and the Central

SOE Restructuring fund, detailed above, shows that these IGFs did not attract any private limited partners and depend wholly on state organizations for funding. In the case of the IC Fund, the biggest contributors are the national budget and the China Development Bank, fiscal and quasi-fiscal institutions respectively. The next biggest is the Tobacco Monopoly (11 billion RMB), followed by three local government-controlled entities from Beijing, Wuhan and Shanghai. It is transparently obvious that these "stakeholders" were corralled into investing in these funds either because they had money —that is, they were cash-rich members of the "national team"— or because they were government entities bidding for a piece of the action. These funds are all disguised fiscal funds or, what is nearly the same thing, funding from the government development bank. The government may choose to allow the Tobacco Monopoly to put funds into the IC Fund instead of paying taxes, but that does not change the fiscal impact of the expenditure. The Central SOE Structural Adjustment Fund shows the same pattern with its enormous contribution from the Postal Savings Bank (50 billion RMB), sending it in the same direction as Japan's ill-fated Postal Savings Bank of decades ago. Meanwhile, China Mobile, one of the world's most cash-rich corporations, seems destined to be called on to contribute to many different IGFs.

Local IGFs will probably have more success in attracting private LPs. However, this reflects the different relationship between government and private business at the municipal level. Many private firms have cozy relationships with local governments. IGFs will quickly become a new way for local governments to extract some pay-back from favored local firms. "Surely, a public-spirited firm would want to invest in our local funds! Especially if they'd like to get some investments from it." This logic is already at work in the national IC fund, where local technology development zones take a stake in the fund, in the expectation that they will in turn also receive investment from the fund. Again, this is not really "mobilizing social capital," as the IGFs claim to do. Finally, a private actor interested in targeted sectors could surely do better by investing on their own, and then bringing one of the IGFs in as a partner, rather than investing in the IGF themselves. Since this is entirely permitted, indeed encouraged, by the rules of the game, it is hard to see why private investors would want to join the IGFs.

5.4.2. Implicit Government Guarantees

The Chinese government induces investment in IGFs by means of a very strong message of government support. This profoundly erodes the credibility of the government's statements that investments will be undertaken on market principles, since it implies that government will stand ready to bail-out bad investments. Indeed, the government explicitly states that it *will* bail out specific types of investors, such as the (government) insurance company investing in preferred stock at the National IC Fund, and has even made provisions for budgetary set-asides for this bail-out. Clearly, the government's implicit promise to bail out preferred stock-holders —but not ordinary share-holders— is based on an artificially clear distinction that is unlikely to be credible in the market-place.

After all, investment managers face obvious conflicts in their decision-making. Although they are supposedly incentivized to make profitable investments, everybody understands that they are supposed to be fostering *national* industry. These funds are not supposed to flow to foreign companies, unless the foreign company makes some dramatic contribution to China's industry preferably in the form of intellectual property. Therefore, the incentives for investors are really not to maximize return. Contrast this with Silicon Valley, where venture capital firms have every incentive to reach out internationally, specifically to China, and create new types of production-sharing, research-sharing and finance-sharing with Chinese entities. Since the objective is to foster national industry, at what point does the investor pull the plug on an investment that is not performing well? What's the budget constraint? At what point does the investment fail? If the investment can be propped up through barriers to competition, the incentive is very strong to do so. Even local governments are susceptible to temptation to support local firms against distant competitors in Shenzhen or Nanjing, and everyone has an incentive to create forms of protectionism against foreign companies. These incentives are deeply embedded in the political economic system in which IGFs are implanted.

In fact, we have seen that the government intentionally diffuses risk and responsibility among a variety of limited partners. Having induced these wealthy public entities to invest, is it credible that the government will impose losses on them in the event of catastrophically bad investments? Probably not. The parties all know the government is the driver. In fact, the government has intentionally created a "convoy system," such as that in Japan in the 1990s, in which all of the biggest firms (*keiretsu* in Japan) supported each other and the government did not allowed anybody to go bankrupt. There is general agreement among Japan economists that the convoy system in Japan contributed to a decade of stagnation when the economy slowed and investments went bad, and it took a decade to unwind investments and get financial channels flowing again. China has now intentionally created the same potential adverse trade-off: in the event of bad investment outcomes, the government will either bail out interested parties directly, or engage in a protracted period in which debts and cross-cutting obligations are slowly resolved.

5.4.3. Soft Corruption

Much attention has been given to the anti-corruption campaign in China under Xi Jinping, which has increased the risks of overt corruption. However, the IGF system creates new incentives for "soft" corruption. Government funds are being channeled into highly risky and speculative investments at an unprecedented rate. Especially at the early start-up phases, venture capitalists expect most investments to fail (but enough good ones to succeed for their profits to compensate for the majority of losers). This creates a huge incentive to channel funds to related parties who then make a half-hearted effort to run "start-ups" that they actually expect to fail. This is already happening. Many in urban China are familiar with cases of individuals running shoddy, flimflam operations supposedly engaged in AI or some web-based platform, but which are actually speculating in real estate or other short-term ventures.

More broadly, IGFs are fully authorized to take stakes in firms that are listed on the stock exchange. Indeed, the dominant form of investment by the National IC Fund in its first round, was to take stakes in existing firms. In the last ten months of its existence (Sept. 2017 - June 2018), the first round of the National IC Fund took stakes in 11 different listed firms in 15 private placements, totaling US $3.68 billion (Integrated Micro Web 2018). These investments in public placements create obvious opportunities for insider trading, especially through front-running these investments. Even after the investment is made, it essentially announces the government's seal of approval on these individual firms. One would expect the risk to decline and the value of these firms to increase —that is after all the whole purpose of the policy— and thus they may be good short-term investments.[13] Individuals should be able to profit from this knowledge.

This point intersects with the previous point when investments go bad. Policy-makers will face a profound dilemma: either write off bad investments quickly (which will acknowledge the implicit government guarantees and reward soft corruption) or try to track down responsibility and allocate blame (which will cause economic slowdown by freezing credit and delaying resolution). These costs will only appear as investments start to fail, but failed investments are an inevitable part of frontier, high-tech investing.

13 This would make an interesting research project, since we have the dates of 14 interventions in the stock market by the National IC Fund.

5.4.4. Investment Bubble

As shown in Chapter 5.2.1., more than three-quarters of the value of IGFs are in those controlled by local governments. Yet only a few regions have expertise in any of the emerging industries targeted by national policy. Since the broad priorities for IGFs are laid out at the national level, the result is inevitably a flood of subsidized money into duplicate projects in many areas. It is inevitable that this will create a huge bubble in numerous sectors, in turn creating a new, and even more widespread, debt crisis. In the meantime, the flow of government money combined with the excitement of genuinely new technologies means that there is pervasive optimism among high-tech businessmen. Even those who are not running government funds are benefitting from the huge net flow of government funding into high-tech sectors. It is difficult to see how this bubble can end, if not in tears.

In the short run, this risk has been deferred because of the apparent acceleration of investment that has occurred in the wake of the US-China "trade war," and the sanctioning by the U.S. of Chinese entities, including Huawei. The reaction of policy-makers has been to step-up investment in semiconductor production, but since semiconductor makers essentially had unlimited funding already, this is unlikely to change the trajectory of policy very much. However, it will ensure that policy continues to support elevated valuations of firms in the semiconductor sector. The long-run implications are like to include a bigger and more dangerous bubble, to say nothing of future over-capacity problems.

5.5. Conclusions

China has been undergoing a sustained bout of institutional creation little noticed by the outside world. Policy-makers hope that the new institutions will contribute to a new economic model, one in which government steers an economy that remains fundamentally based on market forces. Given that policy-makers believe that the new technological revolution is creating a once-in-a-generation opportunity, this steerage will, in their view, help ensure that the Chinese economy will break through to a high-technology future with a much higher level of productivity.

It is unlikely that the institutions created recently by Chinese policy-makers will be as efficient and trouble-free as Chinese leaders seem to think. In fact, as the preceding discussion shows, they are laced with incentive problems that will emerge at a later stage of development. Nevertheless, it is not appropriate to measure these new institutions against a theoretical first-best institutional set-up. Rather, they should be evaluated within the context of the technological revolution to which Chinese industrial policy is increasingly geared. If it is possible to accelerate the movement to a networked, intelligent economy, there could be a large pay-off. The institutional innovations in which Chinese policy-makers are staking so much should be seen as a way of lowering the excess cost of driving the economy toward that technological transition. Some costs are inevitable, since markets can't price in futures that are so complex and uncertain, and a seamless market outcome is unlikely to emerge on its own (i.e., without government action). While not perfect, the imperfections in China's new institutions could conceivably be managed by a government that is sensitive to their weaknesses as well as their strength. In that case, although it is a matter of faith to believe that we are on the threshold of a technological revolution, if that faith turns out to be warranted, the institutional set-up might prove to be a success despite its imperfections.

6

Conclusions

This book has examined and described China's industrial policy, going back to 1978 and taking the story up through 2020. A few simple conclusions have emerged clearly from our investigation. China passed a major policy turning-point in 2006, beginning a steadily increasing commitment to the use of government industrial policy. That commitment increased around 2009-2010, after the Global Financial Crisis. Most recently, with a further shift in 2015-2016, the government launched a new and intensified round of industrial policy under the rubric of the Innovation-Driven Development Strategy (IDDS). This new round is bigger, more intrusive, and more comprehensive than any previous Chinese industrial policy. It is unprecedented.

In examining the IDDS, we have discovered that it is technologically and economically more sophisticated than any predecessors. Technologically, it can be seen as a response to the opportunity provided by a new wave of technological change, a set of "general purpose" technologies that potentially will provide a long-term productivity boost to many sectors of the economy.

Moreover, this type of revolutionary technological change potentially provides a justification for industrial policy, since we have no reason to believe that unfettered market forces will be effective in capturing the spill-overs and complementarities between technological advance in different sectors. Moreover, the dependence of these new technologies on government-provided "new infrastructure" also creates an argument for the government to take a more activist role. Economically, China's policies are less distortionary than previous policies based on administrative instruments. They rely heavily on economic levers such as tax exemptions, and subsidized depreciation and research, to say nothing of the massive Industrial Guidance Funds described in Chapter 5. These initiatives provide the possibility that China's industrial policy will be carried out with lower overall cost than would otherwise be the case.

China deserves credit for these important initiatives. Yet at the same time, there are substantial risks involved in the course that China is taking. Even when markets cannot be relied upon to produce socially optimal outcomes, it does not follow that government can always substitute effectively for the market. Policymakers do not have a clearer vision of the future than individual entrepreneurs, and the ultimate impact of their policy interventions is often very different from what they intended. A discussion of the actual impact of China's industrial policies today is beyond the scope of this work, but we can clearly see that China's policy-makes are creating an enormous expenditure of public funds that might not pay off, and are thus taking on substantial risk. We can identify three overarching types of risk that the policies encounter: technological, economic, and international.

Technological risk is present because the ultimate configuration of the new network and A.I. based technologies is unknown. Being a pioneer subjects China to the risk of investing in second-best technologies that turn out to be expensive and quickly obsolete. What kind of smart networks will ultimately prove most effective in managing traffic based on autonomous vehicles? Which machine learning algorithms will ultimately be trusted to process the choices and mistakes of individual citizens? What will the factories of the future look like? These questions will only be worked out gradually over future decades. Yet today the average per capita household income in China (2019 data) was 42,359 for urban households and 16,021 RMB for rural households. Even at the generous purchasing power parity (PPP) conversion of 4.184 to the US dollar (the finding of the 2017 round of the International Comparison Project), that means that the average urban income was just over $10,000, and the average rural income was just under $4,000. Does it make sense for a middle income country of this sort to be taking such a disproportionate part of the risky expenditure involved in pioneering new technologies? From a purely economic perspective it does not, but of course policymakers have other considerations in mind as well.

Economic risk is present because of the attraction of resources to targeted sectors. These risks were discussed in Chapter 5. Ultimately, the government is subsidizing returns for tens of thousands of uncoordinated investments in perhaps a hundred related sectors. The situation is replete with moral hazard, because the government is offering multiple implicit guarantees which it will be unable to sustain if returns from these investments are less robust than the government hopes. The economic risk could thus be manifest in acute or chronic economic illness. Acute crisis could develop if the interlocking network of investments suddenly breaks down, due to some sudden withdrawal of liquidity. Chronic economic illness will develop if government is unable to liquidate multiple poor investments in which it has a stake, tying up credit and real resources in poorly performing assets and zombie companies. These risks are real, over a 3 to 10 year horizon.

International risk arises from the reaction of other countries to China's industrial policies. Obviously, this risk has already become seriously manifest in the explosive trade war between the U.S. and China and the extensive technological sanctions that the U.S. has already applied to some Chinese companies, such as the telecom equipment manufacturer Huawei. Some aspects of the U.S. response are in violation of international law and appear rash and foolhardy. Yet one can hardly avoid the conclusion that some kind of international backlash against China's industrial policies was inevitable. The world has a complex set of agreements that guard against government subsidies of exports, to which China, as a W.T.O. member, is a signatory. China has been able to sidestep those obligations largely because it is such a large economy that it can provide massive industrial subsidies targeted at its domestic economy in the expectation that these will later, and less directly, subsidize exports as well. As a result, these subsidies do not automatically trigger legal action against export subsidies (defined as a wedge between domestic prices and export prices), allowing China to defend them as domestic policies. Such a situation cannot possibly be sustainable in the long run. Other countries —and not just the U.S.— simply won't agree to a situation where their most formidable competitor (China) is able to engage in a vast range of subsidy behavior that effects their most valuable markets and exports.

It is unclear to what extent Chinese policy-makers have considered the technological, economic, and international risks of their industrial policies. It appears rather that policy-makers have been seduced by the vision of a technological revolution and a substantial re-ordering of global strategic relations and have rushed ahead with an aggressive and decisive round of industrial policies. At a minimum, this is an enormous gamble. As stated repeatedly in this essay, Chinese would in any case have emerged as a technology giant over the next decade or two. It is not necessarily beneficial to have government forcibly attempt to accelerate the process, creating substantial additional risk, waste, and conflict. Indeed, it may end up seriously retarding the global benefits that are potentially available from new technologies, particularly if the world ends up partitioned into competing technological blocks.

Chinese industrial policies are so large, and so new, that we are not yet in a position to evaluate them. They may turn out to be successful, but it is also possible that they will turn out to be disastrous. Obviously, many other intermediate outcomes are also possible. One thing we can say with certainty, however, is that

China's world-shaking economic success cannot be attributed to industrial policy. Quite the contrary, as we showed in Chapter 2 and 3, the explosive growth that propelled China out of poverty to become the second-largest economy in the world was due to deep structural factors and market-oriented reforms. Industrial policy played no role in it, since industrial policies essentially did not exist before 2006. Since that time, they have steadily ramped up, but there have been substantial lags in setting up new institutions and projects and actually making investments. China's industrial policies are unprecedented. It is not yet clear what their impact will be.

References

21st Century Economic Herald. 2016. "Bring into play its superiority in equity investment, the PICC realizes both economic return and social benefit." *21st Century Economic Herald [21 Shiji Jingji Daobao]*, November 25, accessed at http://epaper.21jingji.com/html/2016-11/25/content_51182.htm.

Boeing, Philipp. 2016. "The allocation and effectiveness of China's R&D subsidies – Evidence from listed firms". *Research Policy* 45, pp. 1774-1789.

Brandt, Loren, Johannes, Van Biesebroeck and Yifan Zhang. 2012. "Creative accounting or creative destruction? Firm-level productivity growth in Chinese manufacturing". *Journal of Development Economics* 97, pp. 339–351.

Brandt, Loren and Thomas G. Rawski. 2019. *Policy, Regulation and Innovation in China's Electricity and Telecom Industries*. Cambridge: Cambridge University Press.

Cao, Cong, Richard P. Suttmeier and Denis Fred, Simon. 2006. "China's 15 Year Science and Technology Plan". *Physics Today 59(12)*, pp. 38-43, accessed at http://dx.doi.org/10.1063/1.2435680.

CCP (Chinese Communist Party) Central Committee. 1990. "Decision on Further Improving the Economic Environment". Issued November 9, 1989. Translation in FBIS *China Report*, January 18, pp. 24-37.

CCP Central Committee. 2010. "Party Center Suggestions on Setting the 12th Five Year Plan for Economic and Social Development". Issued October 18, accessed at: http://finance.jrj.com.cn/2010/10/2719488427859.shtml.

CCP Party Center and State Council. 2016. "An Outline of the National Innovation Driven Development Strategy". *Xinhua*, May 29, accessed at http://www.xinhuanet.com/politics/2016-05/19/c_1118898033.htm.

CCP Party Center and State Council. 2020. "Views on Accelerating the Perfection of the Socialist Market Economic System in the New Era." *New China News Agency*, May 18, accessed at http://www.gov.cn/zhengce/2020-05/18/content_5512696.htm.

Chen, Lei. 2010. "Megaprojects are an accelerated icebreaker; a commission member watches tens of billions of RMB in expenditures". *Ribao, Keji* [Science and Technology Daily], March 3, accessed at http://www.cnr.cn/allnews/201003/t20100304_506098012.html.

Chen, Ling. 2011. *System, Elites and Consensus: In search of a new explanatory framework for China's Policy Process* [Zhidu, Jingying yu Gongshi: Xunqiu Zhongguo zhengce guocheng de jieshi kuangjia]. Beijing: Tsinghua University Press.

Chen, Ling and Barry Naughton. 2016. "An Institutionalized Policy-making Mechanism: China's Return to Techno-Industrial Policy". *Research Policy* 45, pp. 2138-2152.

Chen, Xikang. 1989. "Input-Output Techniques in China". *Economic System Research* I, pp. 87-95.

Chen, Yanpeng. 2015. "Uncovering the mystery of the SOE Reform Fund: Where does 550 billion RMB come from and where will it be invested?" *Huaxia Daily*, May 27, accessed at http://fund.eastmoney.com/news/1593,20170527742275031.html.

China Engineering Technology Development Strategy Research Academy. 2015. *China Strategic Emerging Industries Development Report 2015* (in Chinese). Beijing: Kexue Publishing.

China Merchants Equity Analysis. 2014. "A detailed guide to the investments of the National IC Industry Fund [in Chinese]". April 3, accessed at https://www.douban.com/note/549460407/.

Chinese Communist Party and State Council. 2016. "Outline of the Innovation-Driven Development Strategy [in Chinese]". *Xinhua News Agency*, May 19, accessed at http://www.xinhuanet.com/politics/2Xin016-05/19/c_1118898033.htm.

CDB (China Development Bank). 2019. "CDBC Profile," accessed at http://www.cdb-capital.com/GKJR/abouten/list.

Cision. 2018. "Intel and Unigroup Spreadtrum & RDA Announce 5G Strategic Collaboration." *Cision*, February 22, accessed at https://www.newswire.ca/news-releases/intel-and-unigroup-spreadtrum--rda-announce-5g-strategic-collaboration-674831153.html.

Dehong, Guo. 2006. *Historical Surpassing: A Comprehensive View of Chinese Plans from the First to the Eleventh Five Year Plan* [in Chinese]. Beijing: Zhonggong Dangshi,.

Edler, Jakob and Jan Fagerberg. 2017. "Innovation policy: what, why, and how". *Oxford Review of Economic Policy*, Volume 33, Number 1, pp. 2–23.

Fang, Jiaxi and Shen Yang. 2011. "The Country's Financial Strategy for Emerging Industries" (in Chinese). *Jingji Cankaobao* 9, September, accessed at http://finance.sina.com.cn/roll/20110909/013110456623.shtml

Hamrin, Carol. 1990. *China and the Challenge of the Future: Changing Political Patterns*. Boulder: Westview Press.

Heilmann, Sebastian and Lea Shih. 2013. "The Rise of Industrial Policy in China, 1978-2012". *China Analysis* No. 100 (January), pp. 1-25.

Heilmann, Sebastian and Oliver Melton. 2013. "The Reinvention of Development Planning in China, 1993-2012". *Modern China* 39(6) (November), pp. 580-639.

Huang, Tianlei. 2019. "Government-Guided Funds in China: Financing Vehicles for State Industrial Policy". *Peterson Institute for International Economics, China Economic Watch*, June 17, accessed at https://www.piie.com/blogs/china-economic-watch/government-guided-funds-china-financing-vehicles-state-industrial-policy.

Integrated Micro Web. 2018. "The big national fund emerged 15 times in 10 months, serving as a strategic investor to invigorate the sector," *Integrated Micro Web* [Jiweiwang], August 3, 2018, accessed at http://laoyaoba.com/ss6/html/91/n-682291.html.

International Electronics Commerce [Guoji Dianzi Shangqing]. 2018. *International Electronics Commerce [Guoji Dianzi Shangqing]*, July 16, 2018. Accessed at https://www.esmchina.com/news/3822.html.

Jung, Joo-youn. 2008. "Retreat of the State? Restructuring the Chinese Central Bureaucracies in the Era of Economic Globalization". *The China Review* Vol. 8, No. 1 (Spring), pp. 105–125.

Kennedy, Scott. 2010. "The myth of the Beijing Consensus". *Journal of contemporary China*, June 19(65), pp. 461-477.

Knight, John. 2014. "China as a Developmental State". *The World Economy* 37(10), pp. 1335-1347.

Lan, Lin 兰琳. 2018. "Revealing the Mystery of the 'National Team". *Semiconductor Fund, Sohu Finance*, April 27, accessed at https://www.sohu.com/a/229546516_100001551.

Li, Biao. 2018. "A 300 billion SEI Development Fund has been established; it will mainly invest in information technology, high quality machinery, etc". *Daily Economic News* [Meiri Jingji Xinwen], June 12, accessed at http://www.nbd.com.cn/articles/2018-06-12/1225462.html.

Li, Zhenghua. 2010. "Study of the 1978 State Council Theory-Oriented Meeting". *Dangdai Zhongguoshi Yanjiu*, March 17(2), pp. 4-13.

Lin, Justin Yifu. 1992. "Rural Reform and Agricultural Growth in China". *American Economic Review* 82, pp. 34–51.

Lin, Justin Yifu. 2012. *New Structural Economics: A Framework for Rethinking Development and Policy*. Washington, D.C.: World Bank.

Linden, Greg. 2004. "China Standard Time: A Study in Strategic Industrial Policy". *Business and Politics* Volume 6, Issue 3, pp. 1-26.

Liu, Guoguang. 2006. "中国十个五年计划研究报告" [A Research Report on China's Ten Five Year Plans]. Beijing: Renmin, pp. 378-390.

Lu, Hanlu, Amy Przybyla, Lauren Reed, Mengting Wang, and Han Xu. 2012. "A Framework and Case Studies to Evaluate China's Megaprojects and Strategic Emerging Industries." Paper presented at the Conference on the Structure, Process, and Leadership of the Chinese Science and Technology System, University of California, San Diego, La Jolla, California, July 16-17.

Ministry of Finance (Economic Construction Division). 2018. "The operation and investments of the National Integrated Circuit Industry Fund are running smoothly" accessed at http://jjs.mof.gov.cn/zhengwuxinxi/gongzuodongtai/201508/t20150828_1438798.html.

Ministry of Science and Technology Policy Regulation and System Reform Section. 2007. *Guihua Gangyao Peitao Zhengce Shishi Xize Xuanbian* [Selected Regulations for Implementing Policies Complementary to the Long-term Plan Summary Version]. Beijing: Ministry of Science and Technology.

Montinola, Gabriele, Qian, Yingyi and Barry, Weingast. 1995. "Federalism, Chinese Style: The Political Basis for Economic Success in China". *World Politics* 48(1), pp. 50-81.

Mu, Qing and Keun Lee. 2005. "Knowledge diffusion, market segmentation and technological catch-up: The case of the telecommunication industry in China". *Research Policy* 34, pp. 759–783.

NBS (National Bureau of Statistics). 2019. *China Statistical Abstract*. Beijing: NBS.

NDRC (National Development Reform Commission). 2016. "Temporary Methods for Managing Government-Funded Sector Investment Funds," December 30, accessed at cjs.ndrc.gov.cn/zcfg/201701/W020170113678647152209.docx.

NDRC and other agencies. 2018. "Opinions of promoting the demonstration effect of the initial use of technologically significant [domestic] machinery". Issued April 17, accessed at http://www.miit.gov.cn/n1146290/n4388791/c6136528/content.html.

Naughton, Barry. 1990. "China's Experience with Guidance Planning". *Journal of Comparative Economics* 14, pp. 743-67.

Naughton, Barry. 2005. "The New Common Economic Program: China's Eleventh Five Year Plan and What It Means". *China Leadership Monitor*, Issue 16, accessed at http://www.hoover.org/publications/clm/issues.

Naughton, Barry. 2010. "China's Industrial Capitalism: Is there a distinctive system? Can it be a model for others?" *Journal of Contemporary China*, June 19(65), pp. 437-460.

Naughton, Barry. 2018. *The Chinese Economy: Adaptation and Growth*. Cambridge, Massachusetts: MIT Press.

Naughton, Barry. 2019. "China's Domestic Economy: from 'Enlivening' to 'Steerage'", in Jacques deLisle and Avery Goldstein (eds.). *To Get Rich Is Glorious: Challenges Facing China's Economic Reform and Opening at Forty*. Washington, D.C.: Brookings Institution, pp. 29-54.

Naughton, Barry. 2020. "Chinese Industrial Policy and the Digital Silk Road: The Case of Alibaba in Malaysia". *Asia Policy* 15:1, January, pp. 23-39.

Office Circular No. 30, April 11, accessed at http://www.gov.cn/gongbao/content/2006/content_310755.htm.

Oi, Jean C. 1992. "Fiscal reform and the economic foundations of local state corporatism in China". *World Politics* 45(1), pp. 99–126.

Pack, Howard and Kamal, Saggi. 2006. "The case for industrial policy: a critical survey". *World Bank Policy Research Working Paper* 3839, February 2006, pp. 1-51, accessed at http://openknowledge.worldbank.org/bitstream/handle/10986/8782/wps3839.pdf.

Plan Chronology. 1987. *Zhonghua Renmin Gongheguo Guomin Jingji he Shehui Fazhan Dashiji (1949-1985)* [A Chronology of Economic and Social Development Plans in the PRC]. Beijing: Hongqi.

Perez, Carlota and Luc Soete. 1988. "Catching-up in technology: entry barriers and windows of opportunity". In Giovanni Dosi (ed.), *Technical Change and Economic Theory*. London: Pinter Publishers, pp. 458-479.

Reuters. 2018. "China's FAW to invest $260 mln in EV start-up Byton". *Reuters*, May 15, accessed at https://www.reuters.com/article/byton-ma-faw/chinas-faw-to-invest-260-mln-in-ev-start-up-byton-sources-idUSS6N1S200K.

Rodrik, Dani. 2012. "Comments on New Structural Economics". In Lin, Justin Yifu (ed.), *New Structural Economics: A Framework for Rethinking Development and Policy*. Washington D.C.: World Bank, pp. 53-56.

SDI Group. 2018. "The National Semiconductor Investment Fund and Huaxin Investment Management Company". SDI Group, last accessed on August 25, at http://www.sdigroup.cn/companies/detail.aspx?ID=859.

S&T Daily. 2012. "China Successfully Launched Beidou-2 MEO-3 and MEO-4 Satellite with One Rocket Carrier Rocket." *S&T Daily*, 30 April, http://www.stdaily.com/stdaily/content/2012-04/30/content_462080.htm.

Schwaag Serger, Sylvia and Magnus Breidne. 2007. "China's 15-year plan for scientific and technological development – a critical assessment". *Asia Policy*, July, Number 4, pp. 135-164.

Shirouzu, Norishiko. 2018. "FAW Group to invest in Chinese-funded EV startup Byton - Byton CEO". *Reuters*, April 19, accessed at https://www.reuters.com/article/china-autos-byton-faw/faw-group-to-invest-in-chinese-funded-ev-startup-byton-byton-ceo-idUSL3N1RX2CH.

State Council. 2006. *Several Supporting Measures to Implement the National Medium and Long-term Science and Technology Development Plan, Outline (in Chinese)*. State Council Office Circular No. 30, April 11, accessed at http://www.gov.cn/gongbao/content/2006/content_310755.htm.

State Council. 2009/a. "Opinions on Using Technology Support to Further the Stable Acceleration of Economic Development [Guanyu fahui keji zhizhang zuoyong cujin jingji pingwen jiaokuai fazhan de yijian]", March 20. Issued as Guofa [2009] 9.

State Council. 2009/b. "Plan for the Adjustment and Revitalization of the Automobile Industry (in Chinese)", January 14, accessed at http://www.gov.cn/zwgk/2009-03/20/content_1264324.htm.

State Council. 2010. "Decision on Accelerating the Nurturance and Development of Strategic Emerging Industries", October 10, Guofa [2010], No. 32, accessed at http://www.gov.cn/gongbao/content/2010/content_1730695.htm

State Council. 2015/a. "Made in China 2025". Published May 19, accessed at http://www.miit.gov.cn/n973401/n1234620/n1234622/c4409653/content.html.

State Council. 2015/b. "Guiding Opinions on Actively Pursuing 'Internet +'". *Xinhua Agency*, July 1, accessed at http://www.xinhuanet.com/politics/2015-07/04/c_1115815944.htm.

State Council. 2016. "Development Plan for Strategic Emerging Industries in the 13th Five Year Plan Period" [in Chinese], Issued November 29, accessed at http://www.gov.cn/zhengce/content/2016-12/19/content_5150090.htm

State Council Office. 2017. "Guiding Opinions on Further Stimulating Effective Private [minjian] Investment Activity to promote continued healthy economic development". State Council Office 79, September 1, accessed at http://www.gov.cn/zhengce/content/2017-09/15/content_5225395.htm.

Su, Jun. 2014. *Public Policy for Science and Technology: an Introduction* [Gonggong Keiji Zhengce Daolun]. Beijing: Kexue, pp. 295-299.

Tang, Frank. 2020. "China approves plan to boost prominence of state firms, despite complaints from trade partners". *South China Morning Post*, July 8, accessed at https://www.scmp.com/economy/china-economy/article/3092339/china-approves-plan-boost-prominence-state-firms-despite.

Wan, Gang. 2009. "Develop the Newly Emerging Strategic Industry; Seize the Commanding Heights of a New Round of Development". *Keji Ribao* [Science and Technology Daily], November 2.

Wind Consulting [万得资讯]. 2020. "5 Years of New Infrastructure; Complete and Detailed Breakdown of the New Direction". April 2, accessed at https://www.zhitongcaijing.com/content/detail/290131.html.

Wubbeke, Jost, Mirjam Meissner, Max J. Zenglein, Jaqueline Ives and Björn Conrad. 2016. "Made in China 2025: The making of a high-tech superpower and consequences for industrial countries". MERICS *Papers on China* 2, accessed at https://www.merics.org/en/merics-analysis/papers-on-china/made-in-china-2025/.

Xi, Jinping. 2017. "Secure a Decisive Victory in Building a Moderately Prosperous Society in All Respects", October 18. *Delivered at the 19th National Congress of the Communist Party of China*, accessed at http://www.chinadaily.com.cn/china/19thcpcnationalcongress/2017-11/04/content_34115212.htm.

Xia, Xutian and Baoqiang Li. 2016. "MIIT: We've completed the military-civilian industry fusion plan". *21st Century Economic Herald*, December 9, accessed at https://m.21jingji.com/article/20161209/herald/04878ebac64d73201b407f75fdc41de2.html.

Xiao, Yaqing. 2017. "Make state capital operation more prominent; a three-level system of innovation development funds for central SOEs is rapidly coming together". *Xinhua News Agency*, May 24, accessed at http://www.gov.cn/xinwen/2017-05/24/content_5196474.htm

Xu, Chenggang. 2011. "The Fundamental Institutions of China's Reforms and Development". *Journal of Economic Literature* 49(4), pp. 1076–1151.

Yang, Yang [杨漾]. 2020. "NDRC Clarifies the scope of 'New Infrastructure' for the first time; will issue a guidance document" [澎湃新闻]. *Pengpai News*, April 20, accessed at https://www.thepaper.cn/newsDetail_forward_7054170.

Yinug, Falan. 2009. "Challenges to Foreign Investment in High-Tech Semiconductor Production in China". USITC *Journal of International Commerce and Economics*, October. Accessed at http://www.usitc.gov/publications/332/journals/semiconductor_production.pdf

Yu, Q.Y. 1999. *The Implementation of China's Science and Technology Policy*. Westport, CT: Quorum Books.

Zhao, Ziyang. 1987. "Instruction on 'Preliminary Research on Industrial Policy in China". March 21.

Zheng, Meng. 2010. "How the Concept of 'Strategic Emerging Industries" was Introduced," (in Chinese). *Caijing*, September 13, accessed at http://magazine.caijing.com.cn/2010-09-13/110519793.html.

Zhijuan, Gu 顧志娟. 2017. "Policy and Market Together: An Effective Force for Enterprise Reform". *CFBond.com*, November 13, accessed at https://kknews.cc/finance/2v6enk9.html.

Zhongguo Ribao. 2015. "30 billion RMB Hubei IC Industry Investment Fund Set up in Optical Valley." *Zhongguo Ribao,* August 5, accessed at http://china.chinadaily.com.cn/2015-08/05/content_21511324.htm.

Universidad Nacional Autónoma de México
Facultad de Economía
Centro de Estudios China-México

THE RISE OF CHINA´S INDUSTRIAL POLICY, 1978 to 2020

Esta edición se terminó en enero de 2021
Editores Buena Onda, S.A. de C.V.
Suiza 14, Col. Portales Oriente, Ciudad de México 03570
Su composición se realizó con las familias tipográficas:
Minion Pro 7:10; 8:10; 11:14
Montserrat 6:7; 8:12; 10:14; 11:14; 12:14; 16:22 28:32
El cuidado de la edición estuvo a cargo de:
Silvia Jiménez Barba